Decorating Furniture

Découpage, Paint and Fabric Projects

Decorating Furniture

■

Découpage, Paint and Fabric Projects

■

Sheila McGraw

Firefly Books

A FIREFLY BOOK

Published by Firefly Books Ltd. 2002
Copyright © 2002 by Sheila McGraw

National Library of Canada Cataloguing in Publication Data

McGraw, Sheila
Découpage, paint and fabric projects / Sheila McGraw.

(Decorating furniture)
ISBN 1-55297-616-5
1. Furniture painting.   2. Decoration and ornament.
I. Title.   II. Series.

TT199.4.M328 2002   745.7   C2002-901441-7

Publisher Cataloging-in-Publication Data (U.S.)

McGraw, Sheila.
    Decorating furniture : découpage, paint and fabric projects
/ Sheila McGraw. – 1st ed.
[126] p. : col. photos. ; cm.   (Decorating Furniture)
Summary: A step-by-step guide to furniture finishes including
tools and materials, processes and projects.
ISBN 1-55297-616-5 (pbk.)
1. Furniture finishing. 2. Furniture painting. 3. Decoration and
ornament. I. Title. II. Series.
745.7/ 23 21   CIP   TT199.4.M34 2002

Text by Sheila McGraw
Photography and cartoon illustrations by Sheila McGraw
Design by Sheila McGraw and Counterpunch/Linda Gustafson
Page production by Counterpunch

Published by
Firefly Books Ltd.
3680 Victoria Park Avenue
Willowdale, Ontario
Canada M2H 3K1

Published in the U.S. by
Firefly Books (U.S.) Inc.
P.O. Box 1338, Ellicott Station
Buffalo, New York 14205 USA

Printed and bound in Canada by Friesens
Altona, Manitoba

*The Publisher acknowledges the financial support of the Government of Canada through
the Book Publishing Industry Development Program for its publishing activities.*

To my son Graham

ACKNOWLEDGMENTS

Thank you to everyone who worked with me on this book: Lionel Koffler for making the book possible; Pamela Anthony, Melanie Siegel and Pauline McGraw-Pike for their assistance, and for lending their hands for photography. Also to Max Piersig and Jason Wing for their strong backs and sharp minds. Thank you to all who lent their furniture to this project and let me go to town on it, and to those who opened their homes to me for photography. Special thanks to The Paint Depot in Toronto for their excellent advice, their cheerful enthusiasm and their patience. Thanks to designer Linda Gustafson for gleefully knocking heads with me to get it all on paper, and to my editors, Sarah Swartz and Dan Liebman. My appreciation to all the people who work behind the scenes producing and printing this book and to the staff at Firefly Books.

CONTENTS

Introduction

■ 8 ■

Tools and Materials

■ 14 ■

Painting Basics

■ 34 ■

Projects

■ 50 ■

INTRODUCTION

Découpage, the pasting and varnishing of paper cut-outs, was once
relegated to picture frames and table trays. The fragile nature of
the craft meant that it couldn't be used for surfaces that would receive
substantial wear. Times have changed. The availability of protective and
durable water-based varnishes, new clear-drying adhesives, and silicone
treatments for fabrics means that not only can you practice this traditional
art on any furniture surface, but that fantastic new approaches are possible.
Dowdy drawers are transformed by affixing an art poster, rusting wrought
iron is made marvelous with a wrapping of fabric, an undistinguished
wardrobe is reborn a botanical wonder with the addition of leaves and
vines. Virtually any piece can be renovated, freshened, updated.

A Brush with Destiny

Many a furniture painter sets out with the simple intention of slapping a fresh coat of paint over a time-worn piece of furniture, only to have inspiration strike. The surprise result is a beautifully hand-painted work of art, a family heirloom to be cherished for generations. The flat planes of furniture — tabletops, drawer fronts and the like — present endless opportunities for decorative and pictorial techniques, while the three-dimensional form is sculptural in nature, offering many angles for viewing. Painting and decorating furniture is creativity in the round. Often the busy grain of wood, an unsuitable finish, or simply the familiarity of a piece of furniture can obscure these qualities until you stand before it, paint and brush in hand.

If you feel indecision creeping up as you try to decide on the right treatment, determine which type of decorator you are.

If you prefer furniture to be outstanding without standing out, think in terms of soft pastels or neutral colors and understated, tone-on-tone textures and treatments.

If you embrace the attitude that anything worth doing is worth overdoing, consider strong color, over-the-top decorative embellishments or a mixture of treatments for a grand statement.

It's no longer necessary to use slow-drying oil-based paints to achieve professional results.

Using This Book

Whether you are new to découpage and applications of fabric and paper, or are highly skilled in the craft, this book will show you clearly and concisely everything you need to know. Beginners are shown the basics, including which materials to choose, simple and foolproof adhesion methods, and complementary paint techniques, while the advanced crafter will revel in innovative, never-before-used materials and their application. This book is more than a simple instructional guide; we have compiled a wealth of information to lead you through the maze of paints and tools available and show you how to manipulate and combine materials and techniques for wonderfully creative results. Check the *Tools and Materials* section (page 14), to acquaint yourself with the many easy-to-find and easy-to-use materials available at paint, craft and art supply stores. Unless absolutely unavoidable, only low-toxicity, water-based products are used and recommended. Water-based paints have evolved into easy-clean-up, simple-to-use, durable products.

Painting basics such as brush painting, roller painting, spray painting, staining wood and varnishing are covered, as is performing a basic paint job for those who simply wish to paint their fur-

Reading through the instructions before starting a project is like examining a road map. It helps you anticipate what's around the corner.

The toy penguin who appears in the Before pictures is there to provide scale, and is 9 inches (22.5 cm) tall.

niture a solid color. You'll also be referred by your project instructions to these sections as required. They provide a gold-mine of basic, common-sense advice and time-saving tips.

To choose a treatment for your piece, flip through the book to find ideas that appeal to you, keeping in mind that the finished look should complement your furniture and that the projects are in a progressive order of complexity, starting with the simplest and becoming more involved as you go through the book. These advanced projects are not necessarily more difficult; they may simply require more steps, drying times or tools.

Measurements are listed in imperial units, with metric conversions following them. To make the instructions less cumbersome, the conversions are often rounded. A quart-sized can of paint is listed as a litre, for example; a yard is converted to a metre. The projects work whether you use the imperial or the metric measurements. Finally, don't let the toy penguin who appears in the *Before* pictures throw you. This little fellow is working for scale, providing a point of reference. Without him, the size of a cabinet or some other piece of furniture could be hard to judge from the photo.

Test all moving parts of the furniture.

Choosing Your Furniture

Perhaps Aunt Flossie left you a four-legged monster. It's probably a sturdy, well-built, solid piece of furniture – better quality than you can purchase today. And it's free. Instead of relegating the monster to landfill, transform it to suit your decor and get ten or possibly a hundred years of use from it. If you don't have an Aunt Flossie, garage sales and flea markets are often treasure troves of old furniture. Another possibility is unpainted furniture – especially the knockdown variety, which is ideal for painting or staining in multiple colors. And don't throw out that plastic laminate furniture. Even recently manufactured melamine-over-chipboard furniture can be transformed with specialty melamine paints.

Just as the world is divided into cat lovers and dog lovers, it is also divided into furniture painters and furniture refinishers. Refinishers feel that wood and its grain are sacred, and that every stick should be stripped and refinished. Painters, meanwhile, believe that wood is simply nature's plastic, to be transformed into painted masterpieces. The truth is somewhere in between, and this book should help balance

A previous paintjob, like this green, can often obscure the potential of a piece of furniture.

This dated desk, inexpensive even when it was new, can be transformed with a little daring.

Simply constructed wooden tables suggest antique, Victorian or rustic treatments.

the two points of view. Virtually any style, type and finish of furniture can be painted, including wood, metal, melamine and all previously painted, lacquered and varnished pieces. But please: don't paint over genuine antiques or other pieces that have historic or architectural integrity, including classics from as recently as the 1960s and 70s. If you suspect your furniture has value, have it appraised. Often, you can simply take or send a snapshot to an appraiser or an auction house. If it turns out that you own a classic, but the style is unappealing to you, sell the item rather than paint it. Antiques with original paint should be left intact. Original paint on an antique, no matter how worn, adds to its authenticity and value.

If you wish to cut down on preparation time, look for a well-proportioned piece that is solid and has a stable finish. Beware of furniture with worm holes, especially if you see sawdust on the floor around the piece – a sure sign of bugs. When they move in, these boring guests will literally eat you out of house and home. And while you can't expect perfection – the furniture is *supposed* to be old and worn – try out all moving parts to determine the aggravation factor of drawers that bind or doors that stick, especially if the vendor has them taped shut. Remove drawers to check that dovetailing is intact and that the bottoms don't sag. If chairs or tables have wobbly legs, check that they can be fixed. Bypass the item if the legs have already had surgery but are wobbling a second time.

If you are planning to apply a smooth high-gloss treatment, choose a piece with a solid, even finish in good condition. Try the

Unfinished, ready-to-decorate wooden pieces demand finishing.

fingernail test. Scratching with your fingernail should not lift the finish. Pieces with dents, scratches, cigarette burns and water or other surface damage require a busy-looking, low-luster finish to distract from the imperfections. You may wish to steer clear of pieces with water damage that has lifted veneer. Loose or raised veneer must be removed and the scars repaired, a job that requires some skill. And take a tape measure to be sure the piece fits its final destination and can be maneuvered through doors and up stairwells.

When choosing a treatment, look for finishes that will enhance the intrinsic style and accentuate the lines of the piece.

If good design is form following function, then great style is the perfect adornment of good design.

Choose a finish in harmony with the mood of the furniture: rustic finishes or folk painting for simple planklike constructions, decorative treatments for Victorian pieces, and English-country painting for chunky, busy pieces.

TOOLS
AND MATERIALS

This section explains the properties and functions of the tools and materials used most frequently on furniture, from basecoat through decorative finishes. The fabrics, papers and related materials needed for a particular application are discussed in the project in which they are required; for example, information on creating découpage with postage stamps is covered in *Postage Due*, beginning on page 50. If several years have gone by since your last excursion to purchase paint, you are in for a pleasant surprise. Advancements in the technology of water-based paint have led to long-wearing products with low odor, smooth texture, a huge color range, dense coverage and fast drying times. Brushes, rollers, sandpapers and many other tools and materials for applying these paints have been redesigned to keep pace. And alongside the paints and brushes, you'll find innovative supplies, kits and other materials for a huge range of treatments.

Adhesives

STICKY SITUATIONS CALL FOR GENTLE TAPES, SUPERTACKY GLUES AND DEPENDABLE PASTES

GLUE White carpenter's glue dries clear and is extremely strong. Use white carpenter's glue for bonding wood when joining or repairing pieces of wooden or painted furniture. Apply a generous amount to the join and connect the two pieces. (If repairing a piece, first clean out the join with a utility knife or sandpaper before gluing.) Wipe away excess glue and clamp the pieces tightly overnight, cushioning the clamps if necessary to prevent them from denting the furniture. If clamps aren't available, bungy cords can often be tightly wrapped around the pieces. When staining a piece of furniture, stain pieces before gluing, since the glue can act as a sealer on the wood, resisting the stain.

HOT GLUE With its fast drying time and good holding ability, a hot-glue gun is ideal for tacking decorative crafts. On furniture, it can be used for adding decorative detail or for finishing, but is not strong enough for gluing structural pieces of furniture. *When using a hot-glue gun, be careful.* This glue sticks to skin and can produce nasty burns. Some glue guns do produce a lower heat, but also a weaker tack.

MUCILAGE Mucilage is the amber-colored glue used in grade school. It comes in a slim bottle with a rubber nipple on top. Mucilage is the inexpensive magic ingredient used for creating crackled paint – the type that looks like flaking paint. The mucilage is painted onto a dry base coat of paint. While the glue is still wet, another color of paint is brushed over the glue. The different drying times of the glue and paint create the technique called crackle, which works best with latex paint.

TAPE Isolating areas to be painted by taping around them is called "masking." Ironically, masking tape is not a good choice of tape for this purpose. Easy-release tape, available in a light and medium tackiness, has two major benefits over masking tape. Easy-release tape is smooth and gives a crisp edge; masking tape tends to be slightly crinkly, permitting paint to ooze under its edge. Easy-release tape peels off most surfaces without disturbing the underlying finish, while masking tape often lifts paint. The only drawback of easy-release tape is its tendency to live up to its name by spontaneously falling off. The trick is to use small pieces of masking tape to tack the ends in place. Remove all tape as soon as possible after painting, preferably as soon as paint is dry to the touch. Any tape left on for long periods will leave gummy deposits or will fuse to underlying paint, tearing it off when the tape is removed.

(1) easy-release painter's tape; (2) masking tape; (3) white carpenter's glue; (4) mucilage; (5) C-clamps; (6) hot-glue gun; (7) cellulose wallpaper paste.

WALLPAPER PASTE Clear-drying, easy-to-work-with water-based wallpaper paste is the adhesive of choice for mounting large flexible materials, such as paper and fabric, to furniture. Purchase cellulose-based paste in dry form from your paint store and mix the required amount with water. This paste needs to sit for fifteen minutes or more after mixing (stir occasionally) for the granules to dissolve. Begin using the paste when it is a glutinous consistency. Use a large soft brush or a sponge to coat large pieces of paper or fabric, and use your hands to coat smaller surfaces such as découpage cut-outs and leaves. Wet pasted paper often develops wrinkles. These will shrink and disappear as the paste dries. Paper can also stretch and will then require trimming when it has dried.

SPRAY GLUE Available at hardware, paint, office supply, craft and art supply stores, this relatively new product is versatile and fast and offers a choice of temporary or permanent bond. Apply spray glue to the backs of stencils to make a light, long-lasting tack for holding the stencil in position. Spray glue can be used as a permanent adhesive for mounting fabric and posters, although it allows only one attempt at positioning. If this prospect causes anxiety, use wallpaper paste. In upholstery work, use spray glue for laminating foam to plywood, and batting to foam. Spray glue is also used for gluing block prints to a roller for continuous-printing jobs. The down side of spray glue? The overspray you get, and the amount of glue that sticks to your fingers.

When using spray glue, be careful to avoid becoming stuck on your project. This glue is tenacious. It sticks like, well, glue!

Deglossing Agents

NEW SANDPAPERS AND SANDPAPER SUBSTITUTES MAKE DEGLOSSING QUICKER AND CLEANER THAN EVER

COMPOUNDS Furniture with a lustrous finish must be deglossed before being painted, to ensure that the paint will adhere to the surface of the furniture. Very high-gloss or melamine finishes require a light sanding, but furniture that has a stable, non-flaking, low- or medium-luster finish can be deglossed with liquid deglossing agents. TSP or another liquid sandpaper can be used to dull the gloss and remove all grease and dirt. Mix the TSP with water according to the package label. Then, wearing rubber gloves, wash the piece with the solution and rinse well with clean water. Allow to dry overnight before painting.

SANDPAPER To promote the best adhesion possible between the furniture's surface and the primer or paint, lightly sand surface areas that will be getting a lot of wear, using fine sandpaper (220 grade). High-gloss or plastic laminate finishes must be lightly sanded. This is a fast job. Remember, you're only deglossing the surface, not sanding down to bare wood. Sand the surface evenly until it has a dull surface texture. When sanding raw wood, always sand *with* the grain. Sanding lightly across the grain can leave deep permanent scratches. Sanding between coats of paint with fine sandpaper (220 grade or finer) will give a smoother, lacquerlike top coat. When varnishing, sand lightly with fine sandpaper (220 grade or finer) between coats. Don't be alarmed by the cloudy effect the sanding has on the varnish. The next coat will be smooth and clear. After sanding any surface, wipe away every trace of dust with a tack cloth.

Choose the right sandpaper for the job. The grit or grade, printed on the back, indicates grains of sand to the inch. The lower the number, the coarser the texture.

EMERY CLOTH Emery cloth – black sandpaper with cloth backing, and gray-black sandpaper with green paper backing – is produced only in very fine grades. Both varieties can be used wet for sanding metal or dry for wood and metal.

GARNET PAPER Brown in color, garnet paper is the most commonly used sandpaper. Use garnet paper for sanding wood, painted surfaces or plastic laminates. Available in very coarse to very fine grades, it is ideal for virtually all sanding requirements, except for sanding metal.

(1) fine garnet paper;
(2) sandpaper for latex paint;
(3) TSP deglossing compound;
(4) coarse garnet paper;
(5) biodegradable deglossing compound; (6) emery cloth;
(7) tack cloth.

GREEN SANDPAPER Recently developed for use on latex paints and varnishes, green sandpaper won't gum up like other sandpapers do. It is available in fine to coarse grades.

TACK CLOTH A tack cloth looks like a slice of cheese in a plastic bag. Usually it comes with no instructions, one of the mystery materials sold at hardware and paint stores. Tack cloths are an absolute necessity for furniture painting and decorating. Composed of cheesecloth impregnated with a tacky substance, its purpose is to pick up all traces of dust. These cloths work so effectively, you may want them for dusting around the house.

Vacuum up any large quantities of dust. Then, remove the tack cloth from the package, but don't unfold. Instead, use the outside surfaces for wiping, until they are completely caked with dust. Then fold the tack cloth inside out and keep wiping. Continue wiping and refolding the cloth until it is completely used. Between uses, keep the cloth tightly packed in plastic so that it doesn't dry out.

You hate sanding, so why not just skip it?
No one will know. Right?

Manual and Power Tools

TOOLS PLUS COMMON-SENSE PROTECTION
EQUAL PROFESSIONAL RESULTS

MANUAL TOOLS If you are putting together a basic toolbox, the following tools are recommended. Start with a screwdriver, the type that stores several interchangeable bits in the handle. (Some of these have a ratcheting device that saves time, energy and wrist fatigue.) Next are the screws. Old furniture that has been repaired will often have mismatched screws, and no two pieces of new furniture seem to use the same type of screw. In a perfect world, there would be one type of screw, and it would be a Robertson – the square-slot type that stays on the screwdriver. A small hammer is handy for attaching wood trim and hammering in loose nails. Small- and medium-sized C-clamps, for clamping glued pieces, are a good toolbox staple. So are small and large paint scrapers for scraping loose finish, spreading adhesive and lifting stripped paint. A small, lightweight, fine-toothed hand saw is often needed for cutting various wood trims. A staple gun is also useful. Choose one that takes ⅜ in. (1 cm) staples. If you have a lot of stapling to do, consider a power stapler. (See Power Tools, below.) Acquire additional tools as you need them. Reduce frustration by storing tools in a toolbox that keeps them visible or has shallow drawers, as opposed to the type with one deep box where tools become buried and difficult to find. There's a catch, however. For the toolbox to be effective, you have to put the tools back in when you're through.

POWER TOOLS

Very few power tools are required for furniture painting and refinishing. A small vibrating sander can be a handy substitute for manual sanding. Occasionally, a power drill will be required for drilling holes for hardware and leader-holes for screws. A cordless, lightweight drill with a keyless chuck is preferable. Purchase the appropriate drill bits for whatever you are drilling, wood or metal, and in the required size. A drill can also take the elbow grease out of screwing in screws. You'll need screwdriver drill bits to fit your drill. To cut plywood for tabletops or chair seats, use the appropriate saw: a table saw for straight cuts, and a jigsaw or scroll saw for curved cuts. No need to skip a project because you don't have a power saw. Many lumberyards will custom cut wood. If cutting metal, use a specialty blade. *When cutting with any type of saw, wear the necessary protective gear and watch those fingers.* If you have a big stapling job, such as a set of six chair cushions, consider springing for a power stapler.

(1) 9 oz. hammer; (2) tacking hammer; (3) hand saw; (4) screwdriver; (5) safety goggles; (6) rubber gloves; (7) jigsaw (scroll saw); (8) power drill; (9) power stapler; (10) manual stapler; (11) paint scrapers; (12) C-clamp.

Unlike hand-held staplers, most power staplers take all staple sizes. The ease of operation makes the job breathtakingly fast.

PROTECTIVE GEAR

Always wear safety goggles when cutting metal, smashing tile for mosaic, or tackling any other task that can produce flying debris. When sanding, spray painting or using other materials that can produce airborne particles of paint or dust that could be inhaled, wear a paper mask that filters particles. To block both particles and fumes (or only fumes), wear a charcoal mask. For some jobs, like applying paint stripper or other toxic materials where the symbol of a hand turning into a skeleton appears on the label, gloves are an absolute necessity. Choose the heavy rubber kitchen-style gloves for these jobs. Gloves are not a necessity for most paint jobs, but many painters won't paint without them. Latex gloves – the ones that are disposable, stretchy, lightweight and thin – are perfect for painting. Wear these gloves for jobs that can irritate your hands, such as sanding, painting, rolling paint, or tiling. No more farmer's hands and wrecked manicures. If you develop a rash or hayfever-like symptoms, discontinue wearing latex gloves. You may have an allergy.

Buying tools needn't break the bank. Buy only what you need for each job, and consider renting one-job-only tools such as tile cutters or power saws.

Metallics

ANTIQUED AND PATINATED METALLICS ADD RADIANCE

METALLIC LEAF The rich patina of gold leafing is no longer the exclusive domain of the highly trained sign painter or the refinishing specialist. Imitation gold and other metallic leaf, and the necessary components of adhesive and sealer, are available at art supply and craft stores. For genuine gold, try a framing supplier. Purchase compatible products all made by the same manufacturer. Incompatible products can cause chemical reactions that ruin the finish.

Applying metallic leaf is straightforward and simple, and the results are professional looking. The adhesive is applied to the surface area and allowed to cure for several minutes. It remains extremely tacky. The metallic leaf is laid over the adhesive and burnished to make contact with it. Excess leaf is brushed away with a small paint brush. Then the leaf is protected with a coat of sealer. Leafing is available in gold, silver, pewter and copper, all of which can be antiqued or left bright. To antique the leafing, purchase antiquing paint or use artist's acrylics. (See *Postage Due,* page 50.)

METALLIC PAINT As an alternative to metallic leaf, paint-on metal (made from ground ore suspended in a liquid medium), available at art supply stores, provides a dense, convincing metallic finish. Don't confuse these paints with small jars of gold and silver hobby-type enamels. You'll know the right ones if they are displayed with the compatible patinas, sealer and etching fluid. Patinas include green or blue oxidation or rust. Choose instant iron, gold, copper or bronze. The labels on the jars of paint include instructions for using each product. A clear sealer, which acts as a primer, is brushed on first, followed by two coats of the metal. The metallic paint can be patinated or sealed as is.

PATINA Patina is the thin sheen on a copper or other surface, produced by age. Patinating metallic paint gives an aged and refined quality to a piece of furniture.

These treatments are usually applied to molded or carved-looking decorative pieces such as pedestals; however, they are also effective on flat surfaces. Blue and green patinas are available for copper metallic paint, and rust is available for iron. Purchase the patinas wherever you buy the metallic paint. All the patinas are very watery. When brushed onto the

(1) liquid copper; (2) sheet copper; (3) patina blue; (4) primer-sealer; (5) etching fluid; (6) mica gel; (7) artist's acrylic paint; (8) liquid iron; (9) instant rust; (10) patina green; (11) copper leaf; (12) gold leaf; (13) sealer for leaf; (14) adhesive for leaf.

dry metallic paint, they begin their work, almost immediately oxidizing the metal. Apply sparingly, adding more coats to achieve the desired effect. Once the patina has finished the oxidizing process, usually three days, clear sealer is applied. Clear sealer can tone down the effect of the patina and kill the sheen of the metallic paint. It's a good idea first to do a test on cardboard to examine the effects of the sealer on the finish. If you don't seal the patinated metal, the treatment may transfer or be damaged by use.

SHEET COPPER Try hobby shops as well as art supply and craft stores for finding sheet copper. This is the copper that hobbyists use for burnishing. The sheets are as thick as heavy paper and can be cut with heavy workshop or kitchen scissors. *When cutting this copper, be extremely careful.* The edges can be very sharp. Injuries are more painful and annoying than paper cuts. (Wearing a cast-off pair of leather gloves can help protect you.) The cut edges can be sanded dull with very fine sandpaper or an emery cloth. Sheet copper can be patinated with the same blue or green patina used on metallic paints. Before patinating the copper, treat it with an etching fluid, often called metal master, which is part of the metallic paint and patina family. Then follow the same steps for patinating metallic paint.

Metallics are most effective when used as an accent rather than as an all-over treatment.

Paint Products

FAST-DRYING, LOW-ODOR, EASY-CLEAN-UP PAINTS, ADDITIVES AND VARNISHES ADD TO THE PLEASURE OF PAINTING

LATEX WALL PAINT Although the experts at the hardware store may insist you need oil-based paint, just keep in mind that they're probably not computer geniuses either. Times have changed. It is no longer necessary to endure the noxious fumes, glacial drying times and tedious clean-up of oil-based paints. The technology of water-based paint products means long-wearing paint in finishes from flat matte to high gloss; low odor; very fast drying and recoating times; and easy soap-and-water clean-up.

Whether you purchase a can of acrylic paint (plastic emulsion) or latex paint (synthetic rubber emulsion) at the paint store – both types are popularly referred to as latex – expect to apply two coats for solid coverage. Don't be alarmed that the paint is a light color in the can. It will dry darker. Choose a low-luster to glossy finish for furniture. Avoid flat finishes, which show fingerprints and scuff marks. Any water-based paint should be well stirred or shaken before using. Latex paint dries quickly to the touch – usually an hour – but it should be allowed to dry several hours before recoating. Consult the label for precise drying times. Water-based paints remain vulnerable and need to cure for at least thirty days before being washed or subjected to wear and tear.

ACRYLIC WALL PAINT

This paint can be bought by the can at paint stores. Because it is water based, it is generally (but improperly) referred to as latex. Check the label for the actual contents. More expensive than latex paint, pure acrylic wall paint is considered the highest quality of most paint lines. But the reality is that when it dries, it has a rubbery finish that tends to stick to objects that come in contact with the surface for any length of time, lifting the paint (a problem on furniture). A better bet is a combination of acrylic and latex. You'll get the best qualities of both types of paint. Like latex paint, acrylic needs to cure for thirty days.

ARTIST'S ACRYLICS

Originally intended as an alternative to artist's oils, acrylic paint has developed as a versatile medium in its own right. Available in a huge range of premixed colors and incredibly fast drying, their compatibility with latex paint makes artist's acrylics ideal for creative furniture treatments. Artist's acrylics can be used straight from the tube for an oil-paint texture or thinned with water for watercolor washes and glazes. They can also be used for stenciling, freehand painting or texturing. Generally sold in small pots and tubes, these acrylics offset the need to buy a large can of latex paint, which is too much paint for detail work.

MELAMINE PAINT

The popularity of plastic laminate, particleboard furniture and countertops has helped create a generation of new high-adhesion paints, referred to as melamine paints. Unlike most other paints, which lose their grip and peel,

(1) artist's acrylics in tubes; (2) artist's acrylics in pots; (3) colored glazes; (4) latex paint; (5) glaze; (6) extender; (7) shellac; (8) spray paint; (9) primer; (10) acrylic mediums; (11) varnish; (12) gel.

these cling tenaciously to plastic surfaces. Always degloss the melamine surface by sanding with fine sandpaper (220 grade or finer) before applying the paint. Melamine paints vary from store to store. If a label indicates that a primer is necessary, use an ultra-high-adhesion, white-pigmented, shellac-based primer for best results. Allow melamine paint to cure for two to four weeks before subjecting to wear and tear or washing. If melamine paint is not available, latex paint can be substituted – so long as the melamine surface has been de-glossed by sanding and a coat of ultra-high-adhesion, white-pigmented, shellac-based primer is applied first.

SPRAY PAINT

Spray paints are ideal for painting pieces of furniture with spindles or intricate molding. Spray painting imparts a dense, smooth, even coat in a range of finishes from low luster to high gloss. It also eliminates the drips, gaps and sags usually associated with brush painting.

While graffiti may have given spray painting a bad name, this art form created a demand for spray paint that has benefited the furniture refinisher with a wealth of low-odor, low-toxicity acrylic spray products in a huge range of colors. Purchase spray paint at hardware, art supply and craft stores. Also available in spray form are textured treatments such as granite and marble; paints for covering metal or rust; varnishes; and fast-drying, crystal clear lacquers. (See *Spray Painting,* page 44, for more information on the application of spray paint.) For the avid spray painter, special nozzles giving narrow to wide coverage are available at art stores that cater to the graffiti trade.

The durable quality of artist's acrylics, their availability in small quantities, and their compatibility with other paints make them perfect for furniture treatments.

EXTENDER Extender is added to paint to slow the drying time. Use extender when working on a painstaking technique, such as marbling, or when applying a texturing technique, such as sponging, over a large area.

Add water-based extender to latex or acrylic paint in the proportions specified on the label. Both extender and glaze can be mixed into paint at the same time. Extender is available at art supply and craft stores in smaller quantities than what you may find at paint stores.

GLAZE Glaze, a milky-looking viscous liquid, is added to paint to make the paint more transparent, while maintaining the original consistency. Add glaze for texturing and layering techniques, such as ragging, sponge painting or dragging, when you want the underlying coat to show through to a certain degree. Some painters are comfortable adding water to paint to achieve the transparency desired for sponging or similar treatments. Other texturing treatments, such as dragging, require the paint to maintain its viscosity; otherwise the paint, if too liquid, can run together and destroy the intended effect. Add water-based glaze to latex or acrylic paint in the proportions specified on the label. Both glaze and extender can be mixed into paint at the same time. Glaze is available at paint stores in larger quantities than what you may find at art supply and craft stores.

Premixed tinted glazes are available at art supply and craft stores. These are paint and glaze mixtures sold in small jars, saving you the trouble of mixing your own colored glazes. Use these glazes for small projects such as block printing, where a decorative, overlapping, sheer quality is desired.

MEDIUM AND GEL Mediums and gels are acrylic-based cousins of the glaze and extender family. They are available at

Extender and glaze are used for layered, textured paint treatments such as sponging.

art supply and craft stores in smaller quantities than what you may find at paint stores. Mediums are milky-looking viscous liquids that dry clear and are used as varnishes. They come in a variety of finishes, from flat to glossy, and many contain ultraviolet protection to help keep underlying paint from fading or otherwise breaking down under exposure to UV rays.

Unlike water-based varnish sold at the paint store, mediums tend to have a rubbery texture when dry, which sticks to objects that come in contact with the surface. Gels are used for thickening paint or for texturing a painting surface. They are milky when dry and are available in a variety of thicknesses, from light (like glutinous soup) to very dense (like peanut butter). Some gels have additives such as paint, sand or mica to give them color and texture. Heavy gels are durable enough, when dry, to be used for a textured treatment.

PRIMER/SEALER *Primer* is more than just a first layer of paint. It adheres more tenaciously than any paint, providing a painting surface that won't peel and an even skin over the surface to prevent patchiness on uneven and absorbent surfaces. Apply primer before painting or decorating, unless you are antiquing with sandpaper or staining. Stain must be applied directly to bare wood.

Many types of primer are available. Water-based, high-adhesion primers are ideal for most furniture. Primers that are not high adhesion are good for walls, but not for furniture. If you are using a water-based primer on unpainted wooden furniture, the primer may raise the grain of the wood. If this happens, sand lightly with fine sandpaper (220 grade) when the primer is dry. Furniture with a high-gloss finish should be deglossed by washing with TSP, or by sanding before priming.

For plastic laminate finishes, degloss by sanding, then paint with a melamine paint; or use an ultra-high-adhesion, white-pigmented, shellac-based primer before painting with latex paint. These ultra-high-adhesion primers require chemical solvents for clean-up (consult the label). Or simply use a cheap disposable brush and roller sleeve. Shellac-based primer is not recommended for varnished or lacquered furniture because it can eat into the finish.

Use spray primer for furniture with spindles or intricate detail.

Sealers have two uses. First, when painting (not staining) unpainted, wooden furniture, use shellac or another sealer recommended for this purpose to seal all knots in the wood before priming or painting. Otherwise, the knot will discolor the paint. Shellac requires a chemical cleaner for brushes (consult the label). Alternatively, you could use a cheap disposable brush. Second, you'll find that clear sealers are sold with specialty treatments such as gold leaf and paint-on metallics. These are used not only as a sealer to be painted over the treatment for protection, but often also as a primer. Purchase a sealer compatible with the products being used.

Whatever type of varnish you use, always apply it with a paint brush. Rollers, especially foam rollers, leave bubbles in varnish.

VARNISH

Water-based varnishes, often called urethanes, are fast drying, with low odor and easy soap-and-water clean-up. They come in a range of finishes, from low luster to glossy, and many are non-yellowing. Varnish enriches color, somewhat like wetting down your car does, and protects your paint job against cleaners, scuffing and chipping. It is best to varnish a full piece of furniture, though varnishing only the areas that will receive wear and tear is acceptable if a non-yellowing formula is used. Several coats give a rich glasslike finish. Varnish can make the use of fabric, paper and even natural materials such as dried leaves possible, encasing these fragile materials in a durable plastic coating.

Don't view varnish as the enemy. Work quickly, avoid overbrushing and apply several coats, sanding lightly between coats. (See *Varnishing,* page 48.) Oil-based varnishes can also be used. If you find that the very quick drying time of water-based varnish makes application difficult, you may prefer oil-based urethanes. They take overnight to dry and tend to impart an amber tone to the finish.

Many a paint disaster has started on the Sale shelf – a quart of paint with a gallon's worth of tint . . . paint in the wrong color or finish . . . and paint that mysteriously never dries.

Paint Removers

NOT LIKE THE OLD DAYS – GENTLE STRIPPING AGENTS AND EFFECTIVE TOOLS MAKE PAINT REMOVAL FUN (ALMOST)

PAINT STRIPPERS If the idea of paint strippers conjures up visions of vats of steaming toxic waste, it's been a while since you tried stripping paint. There are strippers that smell like citrus fruit, and some are non-toxic enough that wearing gloves is optional. Welcome as these advancements are, stripping furniture is still a messy job, especially if the piece has intricate detail or many layers of paint and varnish. A piece of furniture with either historic or design integrity is, however, worth the journey into slime. Stripping a good basic piece buried under several coats of badly applied paint is also worthwhile, because it cannot be repainted until the many layers are removed. But you can also partially strip such a piece, allowing sections of layered color to show through. This treatment is not only interesting and attractive, but it reveals the history of the piece.

The old way of stripping was called dip and strip. The whole piece was placed in a trough of heavy-duty toxic chemical stripper. This procedure often unglued joints and had caustic effects on the underlying wood. Most strippers today are much more gentle. Choose a gel stripper, which will cling to vertical surfaces. Placing plastic wrap over the stripper can speed the curing time. Just check first that the stripper doesn't eat the plastic.

PROTECTIVE GEAR Paint stripper will destroy the finish on your floor. Do the job over several layers of paper (newspaper is fine), with a layer of plastic or, even better (since some strippers dissolve plastic), an old bedsheet on top. Decant the stripper to paint it on. Pour it into crockery, not plastic. Wear heavy rubber gloves for this job, the kitchen type. Avoid latex surgical gloves unless you are certain the stripper won't eat through them. Safety goggles are also recommended. When you brush the stripper on and scrape off loosened paint, some particles can become airborne.

TOOLS Using the proper tools will make the stripping go much faster and easier. In the first stages of the stripping, a medium-sized paint scraper is needed for lifting the bubbled, loose paint.

(1) stripping brush; (2) rubber gloves; (3) organic stripper; (4) gel stripper; (5) safety goggles; (6) paint scrapers.

Next, a hard plastic stripping sponge, which resembles a block of petrified spaghetti, is ideal to use along with the stripper to help lift paint. When most of the paint has been removed, use a stripping brush along with the stripping sponge. This brush resembles a barbecue-grill cleaner, with brass bristles (they won't rust) on one side and nylon bristles on the other. The nylon brush side is ideal for giving the piece a thorough rubdown. The brass bristles remove the last particles of paint and varnish from any carving and trim, and from the grain of the wood. When using scrapers and other sharp tools, remember to let the stripper do the work. Overly enthusiastic scraping can damage fine or soft wood, defeating the purpose of stripping, which is to reveal the natural, unspoiled beauty of the wood.

Hold it! Don't strip that antique! However worn and beaten-up the furniture may be, original paint on an antique adds greatly to its authenticity and value.

Specialty Products

FROM THE INSPIRED TO THE BIZARRE, NEW PRODUCTS ARE CREATED TO FULFILL THE PAINTER'S EVERY NEED

KITS A tremendous number of kits are available for techniques such as crackle, block printing, marbling, sponging and stenciling. Many of these kits are adequate for the painter, particularly if only a small area is to be painted, eliminating the need to buy large quantities of products that will go unused. However, some of the kits are pricey and don't live up to their promises, with poor instructions and materials that just don't work. Many of these techniques are actually quite simple to perform, require readily available ingredients and are demonstrated in this book.

SPECIAL APPLICATORS Manufacturers are scrambling to keep pace with the demand for innovative paint applicators. Aside from the usual brushes and rollers, there are combs (for creating striping and basketweave effects) and raised wood-grain patterns to be rolled and dragged. Most unusual are rollers that have plastic floral shapes riveted to them, reminiscent of a 1960s-era bathing cap. These rollers are used to create texture by layering similar paint colors, thinned with glaze, with the plastic attachments producing a subtle, semiregular pattern. Various sponges, rags and texturing brushes are available too, as are foam applicators for painting edges, corners and flat areas.

SPECIALTY PAINT Fashion designers like Ralph Lauren and Laura Ashley, who have become lifestyle/interior designers, have come out with signature lines of top-quality water-based paints in painter-inspiring rich colors. These paints are created to complement the housewares that the designers also produce. Although this approach to choosing a paint color may seem excessive to some, others find it reassuring and exciting, trusting that the results will be exactly as expected and that the decor and paint will be tasteful and will harmonize perfectly. Other paint manufacturers are producing innovative paints with unlimited possibilities for application. There are very thick iridescent paints, which are applied in layers with a trowel, sanded and glazed to a glasslike sheen. There are paints with tiny flecks of suspended color, which are made to be layered with similarly toned glazes to produce wonderful depth and suspended texture. There are also a variety of spray-paint effects, including a granitelike composition that comes in kit form. There is

(1) stencil cream paints; (2) stencil brush; (3) texturing brushes; (4) marbling spray; (5) flecked paint; (6) marbling kit; (7) texturing roller; (8) spray granite; (9) texturing paint; (10) synthetic sponge; (11) colored glazes.

even spray-on marble veining, although it looks rather like a mix of hair and mushy spaghetti. Instead of trying to create marble veins with it, the creative painter could have fun with the effect in other unusual ways.

STENCILING MATERIALS Purchase a precut stencil from the huge selection available, or design and cut your own.

To cut your own stencils, buy stencil plastic at an art supply or craft store — the lightweight, flexible blue plastic that is semitransparent for tracing designs — and use an X-acto or a utility knife or small, pointed scissors. Lightweight cardboard can be substituted for the plastic. To execute the stencil, use any type of paint you wish: spray paint for smooth even coverage, acrylic or latex paint applied with an artist's paint brush for a freehand look with brushstrokes, or stencil cream paint applied with a stencil (stipple) brush for dense smooth coverage. The spray and acrylic paints dry quickly, while the cream paint can take as long as a week to dry. Use spray glue to provide a tacky backing on the stencil.

Don't be intimidated by the multitude of new products at the paint store. Many can add substantially to your creative pursuits.

PAINTING BASICS

Most projects in this book will refer you to this section to prepare, prime and, in some cases, paint your furniture with a base coat of paint. This base coat is the groundwork for your decorative treatment.

Step one is the preparation. Virtually every piece of furniture needs some preparation before your new finish is applied, whether you're repairing wobbly parts, removing doors, hinges and hardware, deglossing a shiny surface, or sanding raw wood.

Step two is applying the primer. Most furniture – varnished or painted wooden pieces, melamine pieces, or unpainted wooden furniture – requires priming. Exceptions include furniture with a stable finish that will be fully covered in fabric or paper, unpainted wooden furniture that will be stained, and furniture to be painted and then antiqued by sanding. Each project will tell you when to prime; then you can refer to this section for more information.

Step three is the painting. Paint is applied (usually two coats) over the primer in the same manner as the primer was applied. After the base coat of paint has been applied, the creative and inventive stage of adding decorative effects and treatments begins.

Cats seem to gravitate to the laps of those who want them least. Naturally, they're also drawn to fresh paint. Put puss out.

Priming and Painting

Applying a coat of primer before painting is a necessary step for most projects. Exceptions include furniture to be antiqued by sanding away paint to reveal bare wood, and unpainted wooden furniture to be stained. Primer adheres more tenaciously to the furniture's surface than paint does, to provide a strong bond and an even skin. The paint can then flow onto the primer without patchiness or an uneven texture.

Primer and paint should be applied by the same method. For instance, if the furniture is simple with flat surfaces, both primer and paint should be applied with brush and roller. If the furniture has intricate carving, trim, or spindles, spray primer and spray paint should be used. Don't be discouraged by the streaky, uneven quality of primer when you put it on. Apply primer swiftly and avoid the temptation to redo areas. Primer sets and dries quickly, and reworking will tear up the surface. Once the primer is dry, the furniture can be given one or two coats of water-based paint as a base coat. If your furniture has a plastic laminate finish, use melamine paint for the base coat. (See *Melamine Paint,* page 27.) Before adding other treatments, allow the coats of paint to dry for the time specified by the manufacturer.

Touching wet paint is a universal temptation, so devise strategies to keep yourself away while items are drying. Paint just before bedtime, for example. And remember, mistakes are the mother of inventive solutions.

MATERIALS

The following tools and materials may be required.

- small quantity of white shellac
- easy-release painter's tape or masking tape
- quart (litre) high-adhesion, water-based primer; or spray primer; or, for plastic laminate surfaces, if primer is suggested on the label, white-pigmented, shellac-based primer
- painting tools:
  -paint brush, 1½ in. (4 cm) wide, for
- water-based paint
  -roller handle, 4 in. (10 cm) wide, and short-pile sleeves
  -roller tray to fit roller
- quart (litre) eggshell or satin finish latex paint in the color of your choice
- quart (litre) non-yellowing, water-based varnish
- paste wax, buffing cloth

1 *Choosing the primer*

If your piece has molding, spindles or carved detail, you may wish to use spray primer. (Follow the instructions for *Spray Painting*, page 44.)

2 *Priming removable pieces*

Seal any knots on raw wood with shellac before priming.

Stir primer thoroughly before applying it. Primer should be applied to all areas that will be painted.

Start with removable pieces, such as doors or drawers. Lay doors or other flat sections on supports and mask off any sections that are to remain unpainted.

If the drawers are clean, prime only the fronts and their edges. If the drawer interiors are grungy, paint them with primer.

Use the paint brush to cut-in with primer, painting all inside joins and corners that aren't accessible to a roller. (See *Brush Painting*, page 40.) Then use a roller to prime the flat areas up to the brushwork. (See *Roller Painting*, page 42.)

The exterior sides can be primed if desired, but make sure there is enough space between chest and drawer. (Adding coats of primer and paint to the sides can cause drawers to bind.) Water-based primers and paints dry quickly. Wash brushes when they're not in use.

3 *Priming the body*

Bottoms up. Whatever the type of furniture, from chairs to hutches to tables, start priming the body of the piece of furniture from the bottom. Lay chests and cabinets on their backs and turn chairs and tables upside-down. (If the furniture is heavy, get some help lifting it.) Using a brush, cut-in all corners and places that are inaccessible with a roller. Then roller paint the primer up to the brushwork on all surfaces that you can comfortably reach. Priming the backs and interiors of cabinets, desks and dressers is optional.

Stand the piece upright. Cut-in and roller paint all remaining surfaces. Wash all paint utensils with soap and warm water. Allow the primer to dry.

4 *Painting*

Repeat steps 1 and 2, now using latex paint. Allow to dry and apply a second coat if necessary.

5 *Varnishing and finishing*

Continue, painting and decorating your piece of furniture, or if the piece is to be left a solid color, protect the paint and enrich the color by applying a non-yellowing, water-based varnish. (See *Varnishing*, page 48.)

Attach the hardware.

Binding may occur where paint comes into contact with other paint. In such areas, apply one or two heavy coats of paste wax and buff.

Paint the hardest-to-get-at areas first. There'll be less paint on the painter and more on the furniture.

Brush Painting

In spite of the numerous advances in paint tools and products, the most necessary and versatile tool is still the paint brush. But don't get caught up in brushmania. It's not necessary to buy an arsenal of expensive brushes for painting furniture. Use a medium-width brush with an angled cut to the bristles for cutting-in and for painting flat sections; an artist's square-tipped brush for narrow areas and detail work; and a fine-point artist's brush for freehand, intricate painting. While full-coverage painting is usually executed with a combi-

Creating with a brush adds individuality and personality to an otherwise straightforward paint treatment.

nation of brush and roller, sometimes brush painting is necessary to produce brushstrokes, desirable in many antiquing and rustic treatments. (See *Painting Tools,* page 24; *Specialty Products,* page 32.)

There is no foolproof way to achieve a perfect paint job with a brush. There are, however, approaches to brush painting that will garner a smoother, more even coat with fewer drips and sags. Purchasing good-quality brushes, made to be used with your type of paint, either oil- or water-based, is a good start.

MATERIALS

The following tools and materials may be required.

- quart (litre) eggshell or satin finish latex paint in the color of your choice
- paint brush, 1½ in. (4 cm) wide, for water-based paint
- tube of acrylic paint in the color of your choice
- artist's brushes, medium square-tipped or fine point
- chalk or colored pencil

1 *Brush painting a flat area*

Stir the latex paint. Dip the paint brush into the paint to a level of about one-third to one-half of the bristles. Drag one side of the bristles against the lip of the can when removing the brush from the can.

Lay the wet side of the brush on an open part of the furniture, inside an edge. Brush the paint outward, brushing the length of the area, not the width.

Brush toward and over edges, if possible. If the brush is dragged against an edge, as shown in the photo, the paint will form drips.

Continue brushing, quickly and deftly smoothing the paint. Reload the brush as needed. Keep a constant watch for drips, swiping them away with the brush. Water-based paint sets quickly. Avoid brushing over the same area several times.

Overbrushing will create deep brush-strokes in the setting paint. Finish painting one section of the piece at a time.

2 *Cutting-in*

When painting joins and corner detail, load a small amount of paint onto the brush and use the longer point of the brush's angled tip to coax paint into the corner, dragging the brush alongside the join. The angled cut on the brush suits this technique, especially when cutting-in on the insides of drawers and other pieces with many angles and inside corners. Watch for drips and sags, swiping them away with the brush.

3 *Painting details*

Though spray paint is usually best for spindles and other ornamental work, sometimes details must match the overall effect of a brush-painted piece. Load the brush with a small amount of paint. Holding the brush on an angle, drag it in a downward motion along the spindle, depositing the paint in a long bead.

Quickly brush out the paint to an even coat. Watch for any drips and sags, brushing them out.

4 *Freehand brushwork*

Freehand painting in contrasting colors is attractive on carved or turned details. Position at eye level the area to be painted. Use an artist's brush of a size suitable for the area, and artist's acrylics or latex paint. Thin the paint if needed so that it flows easily from the brush, but is not watery. Try to maintain a steady hand. Keep edges even and end the color at a natural break.

To paint freehand designs, such as curlicues or trailing vines, draw your design first with a piece of chalk or a colored pencil. Use a fine-point artist's brush and acrylic or latex paint, thinned if necessary to flow from the brush. Dip the point of the brush into the paint. With your hand raised (laying the heel of your hand on the table creates cramped shapes), apply pressure on the brush to obtain the thickness of the line desired. Paint the line, using the chalk line as a guide only. Following the chalk line too closely will cause hesitation, resulting in tentative lines.

Rollers are available in a wide variety of sizes.
Choose one that fits the job.

Roller Painting

The roller is undoubtedly one of the most important painting tools, second only to the paint brush. It provides fast, even coverage and smooth texture without brushstrokes. A relatively recent invention, the roller has revolutionized painting. But until recently, roller painting was viewed only as a fast way to cover large areas. New, creative ways of using this versatile tool are now being explored to produce repetitive patterns and textured layering of color. For painting furniture, purchase a small roller handle with removable short-pile sleeves to fit. Buy two or

The smooth texture of a roller-painted surface provides an excellent base for creative treatments such as découpage.

more sleeves, because most are good for only one application of paint. Choose a paint tray to fit the roller. A paint tray is better than a paper plate or other disposable substitutes, because its reservoir and textured ramp provide more even distribution and better control of the paint. First, with a brush, cut-in on far corners and other hard-to-get-at places. Then use the roller to apply primer or paint, but not varnish. Varnish should always be brushed on.

MATERIALS

The following tools and materials may be required.

- quart (litre) eggshell or satin finish latex paint in the color of your choice
- roller handle, 4 in. (10 cm) wide, and short-pile sleeves to fit
- roller tray to fit roller
- fine sandpaper (220 grade or finer), tack cloth

1 *Ready to roll*

To prevent air bubbles from forming in the paint and to remove any loose roller-sleeve lint, dampen the sleeve and rub it as dry as possible with a paper towel.

Pour paint into the reservoir of the tray, filling it about half full. Dip the roller sleeve into the tray and roll it so that the full sleeve is coated in paint.

Roll excess paint from the roller on the ramp of the tray, but don't overdo it. The roller should still hold a good quantity of paint.

2 *Applying an even coat*

Position the roller on a surface of the furniture, inside the edges. Beginning at this central point, roll the paint outward in a triangular fashion, criss-crossing previous lines. This technique will give even texture and prevent a grid from appearing. Don't try to achieve full coverage in only one coat. Excessive paint that isn't rolled out will create stretch marks – an undesirable texture.

Apply moderate, even pressure. Let the roller do the work. It is better to reload the roller with paint than to squeeze more paint from it. Heavy pressure will create railroad tracks – a double line of heavy paint formed along the sides of the roller.

3 *Roller logic*

Roll toward and over edges, instead of pulling the roller against an edge. Rolling against an edge creates drips. As you roll, be on the lookout for drips and either swipe them with a brush or roll them out.

Continue rolling, overlapping each new roller of paint over the edge of the last, until the full surface is covered. Avoid the temptation to reroll a wet section. Water-based paint sets quickly, and rerolling will tear up the surface. Instead, allow to dry and apply another coat. For an ultrasmooth finish, lightly sand the first coat with fine sandpaper when it is completely dry and wipe clean with a tack cloth before applying the second coat. Between coats, keep paint wet by placing the tray and roller in a plastic bag, squishing the bag to eliminate air.

Block printing with a roller creates beautifully rendered, consistent, multiple prints for borders or all-over patterns. Suitable roller-block prints can be found at specialty paint stores.

Be sure to check the direction of the nozzle.

Spray Painting

Spray painting gives smooth, dense coverage to furniture with ornamental carving and texture. The invasive nature of spray paint allows it to go where a brush can't reach, quickly and without drips or sags from brushing. Wherever you spray paint, large dropsheets are required to avoid home-and-garden decorating by default. Only a small portion of the paint coming from the nozzle connects with your furniture. The overspray really travels, settling on surfaces and in tiny crevices. So tape dropsheets together and cover everything that might catch drifting paint. Also make sure you work in a well-ventilated environment to avoid asphyxiating the canary. Spray painting outside is fine, unless it is too breezy. A garage with an open door is

The glossy lacquerlike quality of spray paint provides the perfect foil for painterly brushwork and crisp fabric treatments.

best. Indoors, several open windows, or an open window with a fan, will help. Inevitably, a certain amount of fumes and spray will be inhaled, simply because of the painter's proximity to the spray can. A paper mask will screen out spray paint particles, while a charcoal mask will filter out both paint and the fumes of the paint.

Most sprays don't require primer. But if your furniture has a patchy, uneven finish, spray with primer first. Acrylic-based sprays, available in both low-luster and glossy finishes, are superb for most furniture. Choose a specialty spray paint to cover rust or to add texture. If the local paint store has a limited selection of finishes or types of spray paint, try hardware outlets or art supply or craft stores.

MATERIALS

The following tools and materials may be required.

- dropsheets
- charcoal mask or painter's mask
- one or more cans of acrylic spray paint
- one or more cans of spray primer
- one or more cans of rust-covering spray paint
- steel-wool pad

1 *Getting started*

Attention allergy sufferers: a charcoal mask to eliminate fumes is recommended. If the label indicates flammable (inflammable) or explosive, do not work where there may be open flame, including a flame as tiny as the pilot light on a stove, furnace or water heater.

Using plastic dropsheets, old bedsheets or paper (not newspaper because the ink will transfer to the painted piece), cover every surface around your furniture piece that may catch some stray spray or over-spray.

Shake the can for at least two full minutes. Test by spraying paint on a piece of paper. The first few sprays may appear watery until the paint makes its way up the tube.

2 *Spray primer*

If you use a primer, apply one coat. Primer dries very fast. You should be able to turn the piece of furniture as you work, spraying all surfaces quickly. Allow to dry thoroughly.

3 *Rust-covering spray paint*

If using a special rust-covering spray paint, remove as much rust as possible from the furniture with water and a steel-wool pad. Rinse well and allow to dry. Follow the directions on the label for application and drying times.

4 *Spray painting, phase 1*

Position the piece of furniture upside-down on the dropsheet. (If the furniture is heavy, get some help lifting it.) Holding the can about 10 in. (25 cm) away from the object, depress the nozzle fully, spraying the furniture with a light, even coat. Spraying too heavily will create drips and sags. Several light coats are better than one heavy one. Spray all visible surfaces without moving the piece.

Recoat while the piece is in the same position. Check the label. The recoating instructions on most spray paints say to apply another coat within one hour. If you miss that deadline, you must wait three days to recoat. Apply as many coats as required for dense, even coverage.

5 *Spray painting, phase 2*

Allow the paint to become dry to the touch. Turn the piece of furniture upright and repeat step 4. Continue until all surfaces are covered. Allow to dry thoroughly.

The most beautiful stains can come from unexpected sources.

Staining Wood

The opaque density of paint invites creativity, but don't overlook the effect of stain on bare wood. Simple and very fast to apply, stains appear dark in their liquid form, yet are transparent when they dry. But transparent doesn't mean invisible. Stain not only provides color. As it is absorbed into the wood, it also accentuates the grain and markings. What was a bland, bare piece of pine five minutes ago is now a fascinating and intricate natural work of art. Most commercial stains for wood are nat-

This cabinet, constructed of Masonite, was painted with black acrylic paint. Applied with a rag, the acrylic was absorbed like a stain.

ural brown wood shades. However, dramatic jewel tones, rustic colors or rich shades can be had from berries or fabric dyes.

After applying a commercial stain, protect the surface with wax, oil or varnish. Many stains are available already mixed with varnish or oil – making staining and finishing a one-step process. Ask at your paint store about these mixes. Always varnish natural or bright-colored stains to protect the finish and prevent transfer of color.

MATERIALS

The following tools and materials may be required.

- commercial stain in an appropriate quantity
- fine sandpaper (180 to 220 grade)
- sanding block
- tack cloth
- small quantity of white shellac or other sealer
- wooden stir stick
- paint brush
- rags
- quart (litre) non-yellowing, water-based varnish;or furniture oil or wax and buffing cloth

1 *Getting started*

Start with completely bare wood, free of paint, varnish or glue. If the wood was previously painted and stripped it must be free of all paint residue, and the surface should be lightly sanded to open the grain. Unpainted wooden furniture is often sealed – the result of saws used to cut the wood – giving the wood a slightly shiny surface. Wood that is sealed will absorb stain unevenly, giving the surface a patchy appearance. Sand unpainted furniture lightly with fine sandpaper to open the grain.

Holding the sandpaper flat in your hand or using a sanding block, sand the surface lightly with fine sandpaper in the direction of the grain. (Sanding across the grain can create deep scratches.) Wipe the surface clean with a tack cloth.

End cuts – where the wood is cut across the grain – may absorb a large quantity of stain, becoming darker than the rest of the furniture. If you don't want this effect, dilute some white shellac or other sealer to half its normal strength and brush it onto the open grain. When the sealer is dry, stain the edge.

Using a wooden stir stick, stir the stain thoroughly. Wipe the stick on a rag and double check the color of the stain on the stick.

2 *Applying stain*

Lay the surface to be stained in a horizontal position to prevent runs. (If the furniture is heavy, get help lifting it.) Dip a brush or a rag into the stain and begin to spread the stain onto the wood. Most of the stain will be absorbed.

Follow the fresh stain with a clean rag, wiping away excess. Continue staining and wiping the excess, staining to the wet edge of the previous section.

When the full side is stained, allow to dry. Then turn it over and stain the other side. Continue until all sides of the piece are stained.

3 *Protecting the finish*

The finish of a stained piece must be protected. When the stained surfaces are dry, protect them by varnishing, oiling or waxing. Consult your paint store about the different applications available.

Clear thinking: Varnish in a dust-free setting.

Varnishing

Varnishing not only protects your paint job from scuffing, chipping and the effects of cleaning compounds. It also enriches color and gives a deep, glasslike finish. Some fragile materials such as paper and fabric, when protected by several coats of varnish, can be used in unexpected and creative ways. While it's best to apply varnish over an entire piece of furniture, you may opt to varnish only the parts that receive the most wear and need the greatest protection, such as a tabletop or the drawer fronts of a dresser.

Select a non-yellowing, water-based varnish in your choice of finish, from low luster to glossy. These varnishes are fast drying, skinning over within minutes, a quality that helps prevent dust from becoming embedded in the surface. Water-based varnishes have a relatively slight odor and are easy to

Applying water-based varnish is like wrapping furniture in plastic, making a finish as delicate as fabric tough and durable.

clean up with soap and water.

There are only two rules for achieving water-based varnish perfection. First, do it fast, quickly "floating" the varnish onto the surface with a brush, never a roller. Second, resist the urge to touch. Varnish begins to set immediately, and brush marks, fingerprints and kitty's paw prints are permanent. When the varnish is dry (usually a few hours), sand the finish lightly with fine sandpaper, wipe clean with a tack cloth and apply another coat. Don't be alarmed by the cloudy effect sanding has on the varnish. It will disappear when the next coat is applied.

Occasionally, a project with a special treatment, such as crackled varnish, will call for an oil-based varnish. These varnishes take much longer to dry than water-based ones, overnight compared with a few hours. They also lend an amber tone to the finish.

MATERIALS

The following tools and materials may be required.

- easy-release painter's tape
- tack cloth
- quart (litre) non-yellowing, water-based varnish
- paint brush, 2 in. (5 cm) wide, for water-based paint
- fine sandpaper (220 grade or finer)
- paste wax or car wax, buffing cloth

1 *Getting started*

Use easy-release painter's tape to mask around the area that you will varnish. Varnish must be stirred, never shaken. Shaking will create a multitude of bubbles that become trapped in the quickly drying varnish. While applying the varnish, stir it about every fifteen minutes.

2 *Applying varnish*

With a tack cloth, wipe the piece to be varnished, removing every particle of dust from the surface.

Using the paint brush, apply the first coat. Dip your brush to a level about halfway up the bristles.

Without wiping the excess off the brush, flow on a short, wide strip of varnish, starting near one corner or edge. Brush varnish out quickly and smoothly in the direction of the length of the surface, not the width. Try to brush toward the edges. Brushing against edges causes runs and drips.

Repeat, brushing a second wide strip beside the first and connecting the strips. Continue until a section is complete. As you work, check for varnish that has slopped over edges and is creating drips. Wipe drips away with a brush, rag or finger. Continue across the surface, adding to the wet edge of previous strokes, until the surface is covered. Wash out the brush with soap and warm water.

Have a cup of tea and allow the varnish to dry.

3 *Additional coats*

When the varnish is thoroughly dry (usually about a couple of hours), sand the first coat lightly with fine sandpaper and wipe thoroughly with a tack cloth. The cloudy effect that the sanding has on the varnish will disappear when you apply the next coat.

Apply a second coat. Allow to dry. Sand again and apply a third coat, if desired.

Optional: Applying and buffing a coat of paste wax or car wax over the last, dry coat of varnish will produce a glowing, buttery finish.

Crackled varnish is created by layering gum Arabic over tacky oil-based varnish. The resulting cracks are highlighted by rubbed-in oil paint. Crackled varnish lends a lovely antiqued finish when applied over a découpage of Victorian motif.

Postage Due

A Tiny Bathroom Cabinet
Is Treated To Postage Stamps
On A Gold Ground

The door is the focus of this miniature hanging cabinet. Its plain, blank, vertical format and simple buttonlike knob beg for a rich treatment. The antiqued
gold leaf background glows against the color and historical pageantry
of découpaged postage stamps. Juxtaposed against a dramatic black border,
the door looks like a miniature piece of art.

Read This First

This project consists of four straightforward phases. The body of the cabinet is painted a base coat of black. If your cabinet has a plastic laminate finish, use melamine paint for the base coat. (See *Melamine Paint,* page 27.) Then the door is gold leafed, the stamps are laminated onto the gold leaf, and the door is antiqued. Gold leafing is a simple treatment with glowing results. It is available at art supply and craft stores. Purchase the compatible adhesive and sealer made by the same manufacturer. Other adhesives and varnishes can cause chemical reactions that will ruin the finish.

Stamps, with their classic proportions and recognizable subject matter, are a natural element for découpage treatments. Purchase stamps for découpage at a post office or hobby shop. Choose from new stamps, packages of unsorted used stamps, or specialty theme picture stamps. Specialty stamps are not expensive, if you choose carefully. Finally, the door is antiqued with a sponged layer of thin umber-toned paint.

BEFORE

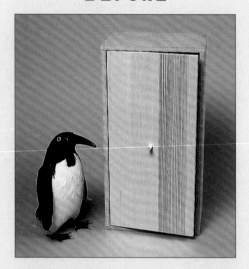

A new, unpainted, wall-mounted cabinet with interesting proportions and a tiny centered knob. The body is made of Masonite, with a natural wooden door. Functional, but bland.

MATERIALS

- quart (litre) eggshell finish black latex paint or acrylic paint; or a can of black spray paint
- gold leaf with compatible adhesive and sealer
- ½ in. (1.25 cm) wide square-tipped artist's brush or a small foam brush
- small house-painting brush
- postage stamps
- ruler and pencil
- glue stick, craft glue or spray glue
- tube of acrylic paint (burnt umber), or substitute latex paint (deep brown)
- sponge or rag
- *optional:* non-yellowing, water-based varnish

1 *Painting the base coat*

Remove the door from the cabinet, if possible. Paint the outside of the body of the cabinet using black latex, acrylic or spray paint. Painting the inside is optional. (This cabinet, constructed of Masonite, was painted with black acrylic paint. Applied with a rag, the acrylic was absorbed like a stain.)

Paint the back of the door. The back and edges of this door were spray painted.

Optional: When the paint is dry, apply non-yellowing, water-based varnish. (See *Varnishing,* page 48.)

2 *Gold leaf adhesive*

With the door right-side-up, use the square-tipped artist's brush or small foam brush to paint the surface with the gold leaf adhesive. Do the edges of the door, unless the door is a tight fit. This adhesive is quite thick, and brushstrokes will show in the gold leaf. Let the adhesive set according to the directions on the label. Apply a second coat, if suggested on the label.

3 *Applying gold leaf*

Lift a full sheet of gold leaf from the folio. It is very thin and may crinkle, which is okay.

Beginning at one edge of the door, lay a sheet of gold leaf onto the adhesive, wrapping it over the edge (if you are doing the edges).

Burnish the gold leaf with your fingers, or lay a piece of paper overtop and burnish it with your hand to make sure the gold leaf adheres firmly. Cracks are desirable in the gold leaf.

Using a small house-painting brush, whisk away all excess bits of gold leaf that are not stuck. This is a surprisingly messy job that creates fairy dust in your work area. Place a scrap piece of gold leaf on any missed areas and burnish. Continue until the full surface is covered.

4 *Découpaging stamps*

Position and mark the postage stamps on the door.

Glue the stamps in place using a glue stick, craft glue or spray glue.

5 Sealing

Using the compatible gold leaf sealer, paint over all of the gold leaf surfaces, including the stamps. Allow to dry.

6 Antiquing

Antique the door. Mix burnt umber artist's acrylics or deep-brown latex paint with water, to achieve a thin consistency. Using a sponge or rag, apply the paint over the surface of the door, wiping away excess with a damp rag. Allow to dry and apply another coat of the sealer over the antiquing.

7 Finishing

Attach all hardware and the door.

*While intricate découpage adds interest, using large-scale motifs adds drama. **Above,** bold fabric is laminated to plywood for a table insert. **Left,** dried leaves are découpaged on a wardrobe. All forms of découpage must be sealed. (See Material Pleasures, page 68; Botanical Design, page 104.)*

Prints Charming

SOFT HUES COMBINE WITH COLOR COPIES OF FLORAL FABRIC TO CREATE ROMANCE

Victorian treatments create the most impressive transformations,
taking the bland and the broken-down to new heights in a glorious melange
of muted florals and classic filigree. A wardrobe lends itself well to a
Victorian makeover. The various surfaces present options for mirror and
glass, fabric details, and a myriad of hardware selections: drawer pulls,
knobs and hinges in porcelain, brass and painted wood.

Read This First

The splendidly decorative results of this project are the product of a few elementary techniques – paint and découpage, plus an added shirred curtain. Select the fabric for the curtain first. Then make color photocopies from the curtain fabric. The photocopies will be découpaged onto drawer fronts. Paint the body of the wardrobe in one shade. Paint the drawer fronts and other areas to be découpaged in a color that matches the background color of the photocopies, not the fabric. (The copying process can alter colors.) These paint colors are the base coat. If your wardrobe has a plastic laminate finish, use melamine paint. (See *Melamine Paint,* page 27.) The curtain requires minimal sewing – only four straight seams. New hardware and a purchased wooden craft bow add sparkle and polish. The results are astounding.

MATERIALS

- fabric for shirred curtain (steps 6 and 7)
- color photocopies of the fabric to fit drawer and door fronts
- quart (litre) high-adhesion, water-based primer
- quart (litre) eggshell finish latex paint for doors and drawers of wardrobe (Choose a paint color to match the background color of the photocopies.)
- quart (litre) eggshell finish latex paint for body of wardrobe (Choose a paint color to match a color in the print of the fabric.)
- painting tools: paint brush, small roller, roller tray
- small, sharp scissors
- tracing paper, pencil, tape
- small quantity cellulose-based wallpaper paste
- quart (litre) non-yellowing, water-based varnish
- sewing materials
- hardware for shirred curtain (consists of 2 rods, 4 hook brackets, 8 screws)
- *optional:* glass or mirror cut to fit (screen or chicken wire, wire cutters and a stapler can be substituted), wooden trim, hammer and finishing nails
- *optional:* wooden decoration, such as a bow, from a craft store

BEFORE

Can this severely water-damaged and weathered wardrobe be saved? Rehabilitation was worth a try. Loose varnish was scraped off. Panels were glued and nailed, and separated veneer was reglued and covered with trim.

1 *Painting the wardrobe*

Refer to *Painting Basics* (page 34) and prepare the wardrobe, repairing it but not yet replacing the glass or mirror.

Prime the full wardrobe and allow to dry. Paint the doors and drawers of the wardrobe to match the background color of the photocopies of the curtain fabric.

Paint the body of the cabinet in the second color.

2 *Cutting for découpage*

Using small, sharp scissors, cut out the photocopies for découpage, cutting as close to the images as possible.

Make a template to help center the découpage cut-outs on drawer fronts. Position one cut-out image onto the center of a drawer front. Position a sheet of tracing paper to cover the bottom half of the drawer front and half the image. Tack the paper in place with tape. On the tracing paper, trace around the half-image and mark the sides and bottom of the drawer front.

Cut out the traced half-image from the tracing paper, along your lines, discarding the cut-out and reserving the background.

3 *Découpaging*

Mix a small amount of wallpaper paste in a bowl, following the manufacturer's instructions. Position the tracing paper template on one drawer, lining up the sides and bottom as marked. Using your hands, apply wallpaper paste to both sides of the image. Make sure there are no dry spots.

Lay the image onto the drawer front, fitting it to the template cut-out. Lift off the template. Smooth the photocopy from the center to the edges. Don't rub too hard or the surface image of the photocopy may rub off.

Allow the découpage to dry. Though small wrinkles may appear in the photocopy while it is wet, these will flatten out (honest!) as the paper dries and shrinks. Do not touch.

Repeat on all remaining drawers. Découpage any other areas as desired.

4 *Varnishing*

When the découpage is thoroughly dry, protect the paint and enrich the color by varnishing the full wardrobe. Varnish all découpaged areas with at least two coats of non yellowing, water-based varnish. (See *Varnishing,* page 48.)

5 *Installing a window*

Install new glass or mirror panels where needed. Lay the door flat, upside-down. Place the cut glass into the window-well on the wrong side of the door.

Screen or chicken wire suits rustic wardrobes. It was originally used instead of expensive glass and allowed air circulation while keeping out bugs and mice. Place the screen in the window and staple it in the window-well. Keep the screen/chicken wire taut and even. Trim any excess with wire cutters.

Cut lengths of narrow trim to fit the top, sides and bottom. Paint the trim to match the door. Position the trim tightly against the glass, and nail it in place with finishing nails. For a professional-looking job, sink the nail heads, fill holes with wood filler and touch up with paint.

6 *Sewing the curtain*

Make the shirred curtain. Measure and attach two hooks (the hooks point upward) to the inside-top of the door. Place the hooks slightly wider than the window and at least 1 in. (2.5 cm) above the glass. Placing the rod on the hooks can help with positioning.

Cut fabric twice the width of the window.

Cut the top end square. Cut the length of the fabric at least 6 in. (15 cm) longer than the window.

Sew narrow hems along each side. Check if the fabric has a pattern that has a right-way-up, such as vines climbing a trellis. Sew a 1 in. (2.5 cm) channel along the top edge.

7 *Hanging the curtain*

Gather the top channel onto the rod and place the rod onto the hooks. To determine the length of the fabric, mark with a pin, 2 in. (5 cm) below the bottom of the window. Remove the curtain from the rod. Add 1½ in. (4 cm) beyond the marker pin, and cut across the fabric at this measurement. Sew a 1 in. (2.5 cm) channel across the bottom.

Gather the fabric back onto the top rod and place the rod onto the hooks again. Gather the fabric onto the remaining rod through the bottom channel. Position the remaining hooks through the rod (hooks pointed downward). Pull the rod gently, positioning the hooks and screwing them into place.

Note: If you wish to remove the curtain easily from the rods, move the bottom hooks high enough to allow the rod to be removed. The trade-off for this convenience is a baggy curtain instead of a taut one.

8 *Finishing*

Hang the doors and attach the hardware.

Optional: A suitable wooden decoration, purchased at a craft store, will add to the Victorian effect. This bow was painted in the wardrobe colors and attached to the top-front with L-shaped brackets.

If you love the fresh effect of shirred fabric on furniture, consider halters instead of backrest cushions for chairs. (See Floral Arrangements, page 92.)

Letter Perfect

DÉCOUPAGE TRANSFORMS A WRITING DESK
INTO A FANCIFUL TREASURE

Charming and inviting, découpage of wrapping paper with deep-forest green
paint accentuates this desk's detail and molding, while providing a cozy
English-country atmosphere. A lucky find of specialty wrapping paper with
Sunday afternoon letter-writing motifs — postage stamps, typewriters, teapots
and clocks — was used to découpage this desk. If similar motifs are hard to
locate, real postage stamps mixed with old postcards from flea markets, or
even old letters — positioned at random — make a
quirky and eclectic substitute.

Read This First

The desk is painted with a color to coordinate with the decoupaged materials. Areas to be decoupaged are left white, because color, especially deep color, can show through the paper. If your desk has a plastic laminate finish, use melamine paint. (See *Melamine Paint,* page 27.) Then two types of decoupage are applied. The drawer fronts are completely covered with sheets of paper, while the desktop is treated to traditional decoupage, with carefully cut-out images pasted on in a random pattern. The background of the desktop is painted to match the background of the decoupage paper, making the cutting-out stage fast and easy. The instructions call for wallpaper paste to adhere the decoupage. Those who are brave can avoid this gooey step and use spray glue. Read the glue can's directions for permanent adhesion, and remember that spray glue allows only one chance to position the image, and no opportunity to remove it. Wallpaper paste is more forgiving. All decoupage must be varnished for protection.

BEFORE

A well-built, solid wood writing desk with interesting feet and trim. The badly scarred top finish and loose base trim provide a good opportunity for a decoupage cover-up.

MATERIALS

- for découpage: wrapping paper, or posters, or paper items such as stamps, postcards, pictures and letters
- quart (litre) high-adhesion, water-based primer
- easy-release painter's tape
- quart (litre) eggshell finish latex paint for base coat, to coordinate with découpage materials
- painting tools: brush, small roller, tray
- latex or acrylic paint for desktop, to match background of découpage pictures (step 2)
- small, sharp scissors
- small quantity of cellulose-based wallpaper paste
- small, soft paint brush; household sponges
- X-acto knife and ruler
- fine-point artist's brush
- quart (litre) non-yellowing, water-based varnish
- fine sandpaper (220 grade), tack cloth

1 *Painting the base coat*

Refer to *Painting Basics* (page 34). Prime the desk with high-adhesion primer and allow it to dry.

Using easy-release painter's tape, mask off areas to be découpaged, such as the drawer fronts and the top, so that they will not be painted. Otherwise, the paint color could show through the découpage paper and give the découpage a muddy appearance.

Paint the desk with the coordinating color of latex paint. Allow to dry and remove the tape.

2 *Random découpage*

To découpage the desktop with small random images, mask around the edges of the desktop. Paint the desktop a color to match the background of the wrapping paper.

Here the background was painted a cream shade and sponged with a warm brick tone.

Using small, sharp scissors, cut out the images from the wrapping paper, cutting as close to the images as possible. Or use other paper images such as postage stamps and postcards.

Position the images on the desktop. Mix some wallpaper paste. Follow the instructions on the container, but mix only a small fraction of the total package. Use the sponge or your hands to apply paste to both sides of an image, leaving no dry spots.

Lay the pasty image onto the desktop. Gently smooth the image from the center to the sides, using a damp sponge. Don't scrub – the surface printing could rub off. Paste all images down and allow them to dry. Sometimes the paper will wrinkle, but don't smooth it out. It will shrink and flatten as it dries. Lifting or rubbing will tear and crease the paper.

3 *Sheet découpage*

Découpage the drawer fronts. Since drawer sizes can vary, measure all the drawer fronts. Using a ruler and a sharp X-acto knife, measure, mark and cut out squares of wrapping paper to fit the drawers, keeping in mind the placements of images.

Mix some wallpaper paste. Follow the instructions on the container, but mix only a small fraction of the total package. Use the sponge or paint brush to apply an even coat of paste (avoid blobs) onto a drawer front, then onto both sides of the image. There should be no dry spots.

Position the paper onto the drawer front. Start at one corner, line up an adjacent side, and then lay the paper flat. Gently smooth the surface with a damp sponge, pushing out any air pockets. Start at the center and work out to the edges. Don't scrub. The printed image could rub off.

The paper may have stretched but that's normal, so don't be alarmed. Let it dry. It will be trimmed later. Attempting to trim it while wet will produce a ragged edge.

Although the paper has been smoothed, it may become wrinkly. The wrinkles will go away as the paper dries, shrinking and tightening in the process. Trying to stretch or smooth the paper will tear or crease it. Allow the paste to dry.

4 *Trimming*

If the paper stretched, or if your measurements were slightly off, the paper may turn out to be too big for the drawer front. When the paper is thoroughly dry, trim off the excess using the X-acto knife and ruler. Use a new, sharp blade. Instead of trying to cut through in one slice, make several light cuts along one line. The blade will be less likely to slip off course.

5 *Finishing*

Using a fine-point artist's brush, make any needed touch-ups.

Apply varnish to the découpaged surfaces of the desk. Découpaged surfaces must be varnished for protection. If you wish, varnish the full desk. Using the non-yellowing, water-based varnish, apply two coats. Sand lightly with fine sandpaper after the second coat. Wipe away dust with a tack cloth and apply another coat. (See *Varnishing*, page 48.)

Découpage can be done on a large scale. When a full-sized art poster is used, straddling all the drawers of a dresser, it creates tremendous impact. Use this technique on a dresser as shown, or on a cabinet with plain doors. (See Posterity, page 86.)

Material Pleasures

FABRIC PANELS ADD DRAMA WITH TEXTURE AND COLOR

There is no better way to dramatically change the mood and appearance of a piece of furniture than to introduce fabric into the renovation equation. Coordinating paint and fabric covers the decorating bases of color, pattern and texture. The extensive selection of fabric — in a variety of weaves and a full range of colors, designs and patterns to suit any mood — means easy-to-make, impressive renovations. Shown here are two very different results from the same treatment, both with fabric panels replacing glass.

Read This First

This treatment is straightforward. The base of the piece of furniture is painted to coordinate with the fabric. If your table has a plastic laminate finish, use melamine paint. (*See Melamine Paint,* page 27.) While the paint dries, the fabric is laminated to a plywood board with spray glue, then varnished for protection. Spray glue allows only one chance to position the fabric onto the plywood when laminating. If this prospect makes you nervous, use wallpaper paste. (See *Office Romance,* page 98.) The panel is then assembled with the painted furniture. Purchase plywood that is the correct thickness for the opening. Cut it yourself,

or have it cut to fit the opening in the piece of furniture. Many lumberyards offer this service. The fit should not be tight, allowing space for the fabric to wrap over the edges. The plywood should be good one side, which means there should be no knots or roughness on one side of it. Good both sides, which is much more expensive, is not required. Check that the plywood is not warped. Purchase enough fabric to cover the plywood piece with a 2 in. (5 cm) overlap on all sides. When choosing the fabric, check how the pattern will fit the panel. Select relatively smooth fabric of a medium weight.

BEFORE

Left, a sorry coffee table with scuffed wood-grain melamine over particleboard and missing glass. Worth saving? We thought we'd try. **Right,** *a charming butler's table, complete with spray-painted gold glass and crumbling, flaking varnish.*

MATERIALS

- quart (litre) high-adhesion, water-based primer
- quart (litre) latex paint, in a color to match or coordinate with the fabric (eggshell or satin finish)
- plywood, good one side, cut to fit panel
- fine sandpaper (220 grade), tack cloth
- fabric to cover plywood, with at least 2 in. (5 cm) extra on all sides
- iron, scissors
- easy-release painter's tape, 2 in. (5 cm) wide
- spray glue (or cellulose-based wallpaper paste)
- dropsheet
- quart (litre) non-yellowing, water-based varnish
- *optional:* saws to cut plywood (step 2)
- *optional:* dressmaker's pins
- *optional:* wood trim and finishing nails
- *optional:* contrasting paint for trim
- *optional:* screws or white carpenter's glue, thick phone book, tools for attaching panel
- *optional:* braid, hot-glue gun

1 *Painting*

Refer to *Painting Basics* (page 34). Prepare, prime and paint the table with two coats of the latex paint.

Paint the piece of plywood on both sides with primer. Priming one side may cause warping, especially if the plywood is thin.

Note: Plywood may be primed and painted before or after cutting it to size.

2 *Plywood*

If it's not already cut, cut the plywood to the correct size or shape. For curves, use a jigsaw or scroll saw. Straight cuts should be made with a table saw. Lightly sand the cut edges and the top (the smooth side), removing any bumps. Even small bits of debris will dimple the fabric. Wipe with a tack cloth.

3 *Cutting fabric*

Iron the fabric, then lay it wrong-side-up on a flat surface.

Center the plywood onto the design of the fabric.

Note: If it is difficult to position fabric on its wrong side because the design is faint, turn the material over. Center the plywood on the right side, marking the corners with pins. Then turn the fabric to the wrong side, position the plywood inside the pins and remove the pins.

To mark a uniform overlap of fabric and supply a cutting line, tape the easy-release painter's tape onto the fabric, around the perimeter of the plywood. On a curved edge, use several short pieces to conform to the curve. Cut the fabric along the *outside* edge of the tape. Don't remove the tape.

4 *Laminating fabric*

Remove the plywood from the fabric, keeping the tape in place. Read the instructions on the spray glue for making a permanent bond. Usually they say to coat one surface well and bond the items while the glue is still "aggressively tacky." Place the fabric right-side-down onto a dropsheet to catch any overspray, and spray the fabric with the spray glue.

Place the smooth side of the plywood onto the glued area of the fabric, inside the taped edge, by placing the point of one corner in position, lining up the adjoining side and slowly lowering the plywood onto the fabric.

Optional: Using spray glue for laminating gives you only one try at positioning the fabric. If this idea is too scary, use wallpaper paste. (See *Office Romance*, page 98.)

5 *Laminating edges*

Turn the board over with the fabric attached. With clean hands, start in the center and work toward the edges, smoothing the fabric onto the plywood.

Turn the plywood and fabric upside-down again. Remove the tape. Cut across the corners so they will meet neatly when they are folded over. If the plywood has a curved edge, cut V shapes into the excess fabric so it will conform and lie flat when folded to the back of the plywood.

Working in sections, spray one fabric edge at a time with the spray glue, then pull the edge gently but firmly onto the back of the wood and smooth it down. Continue until all sides are glued down. Allow to dry.

6 *Varnishing*

To seal and protect the fabric, apply a coat of the water-based varnish and allow it to dry. Apply a second coat and allow it to dry. (See *Varnishing*, page 48.)

Using a fine sandpaper, *lightly* sand the second coat of varnish. Wipe clean with a tack cloth. Don't be alarmed by the cloudy appearance of the varnish.

Apply two more coats of varnish, sanding and wiping between coats. By now the surface of the fabric should be smooth and completely covered and protected by the varnish. Apply more coats if you wish.

7 *Details*

Optional: Highlight wood trim with contrasting color. Attach trim or other details, and paint as desired.

8 *Finishing*

If the bottom of the panel is visible, paint the exposed plywood on the back of the panel in the same color as the table.

Attach the panel to your piece of furniture. The coffee table panel was inserted from below with wood pieces screwed into the table for support.

The top of the butler's table can be simply set in, or glued in place with carpenter's glue. If gluing, place a telephone book on the tabletop until the glue is dry.

Note: If the fit of the panel shows gaps, you may wish to glue braid around the edge. Use a hot-glue gun. *Be careful not to burn your fingers, especially if you are not experienced with a glue gun.* The glue becomes hot enough to cause deep burns, and the glue sticks and keeps burning. Tuck and glue the ends of the braid between the panel and the edge.

Heaven Sent

DIVINE CHERUBS ARE FRAMED BY GILT-EDGED DECORATIVE PLASTERWORK

Every house has room for a little opulence, a lovely departure from the
ordinary, with ever-popular angel paintings in the 19th century romantic style
cut into pleasing ovals of various sizes and framed with a poetic frieze of
faux-plaster relief. Combined with gold-burnished sage green paint, this
heavenly treatment creates a moody yet surprisingly neutral effect.

Read This First

Silicone caulking, the kind used around windows and bathtubs, is the surprising modern material used to create decorative faux plaster work. Choose paintable caulking in a silicone-based product. Silicone has the best adhesion. Buy caulking that comes in a tube with a nozzle and fits into a gun — not the little plastic packages for bathtubs. Don't be intimidated by the gun. After a few practice tries, you'll have the hang of it. Pages from an oversized color calendar of Bouguereau paintings capture the high romance of angels. For découpage pictures, select posters or calendars. These pictures are usually beautifully printed on heavy paper. The heavy paper would normally render it unsuitable for découpage, but in this instance it will be edged in silicone to disguise the cut edge. This treatment should be limited to furniture other than tabletops, where the raised decoration would topple glasses and be harmed by wear and tear.

MATERIALS

- quart (litre) high-adhesion, water-based primer
- painting tools: paint brush, small roller, roller tray
- printed calendar or poster pictures
- access to photocopier
- scissors or X–acto knife
- pencil
- tape measure or ruler
- cellulose-based wallpaper paste
- sponge, rags
- tube of *paintable* silicone caulking, caulking gun
- wire or other narrow, sharp object
- cardboard or scrap piece of wood
- yardstick or other straight edge
- quart (litre) eggshell or satin finish latex paint, in a bone or sage green shade
- inexpensive square-tipped artist's brush
- fine-point artist's brush
- tube of acrylic (or substitute latex) for antiquing, burnt umber or deep olive green
- tube of acrylic, iridescent gold
- quart (litre) non-yellowing, water-based varnish

BEFORE

A 1950s dresser with simple lines and a highly lacquered finish that has seen its share of spills and cigarette burns. Repairing the surface would never be perfect, so a Victorian disguise was undertaken.

1 *Priming*

Refer to *Painting Basics* (page 34). Prepare and prime the dresser, but do not paint it. If your dresser has a mirror, remove it, but don't forget to work on it at each appropriate step.

2 *Cutting oval images*

Photocopy the pattern for the oval template (page 79), reducing or enlarging the pattern to fit the top and the drawer fronts of your dresser. Cut out the center of the oval pattern and trace the oval onto the calendar (or poster) image, making four very small marks on the edge of the picture at the cross lines. Cut out the calendar images along your line.

Mark the positions for the oval pictures on the dresser by measuring and lightly marking a cross at the center point of where a picture is desired. Match the four marks on the oval to the lines of the cross.

3 *Découpage*

Following the manufacturer's instructions, mix a small bowl of the wallpaper paste. Gently rub paste onto both sides of a paper oval, covering it thoroughly. Position the oval onto the dresser.

Using a damp sponge, smooth the image from the center outward, eliminating air bubbles and wiping away excess paste. Do not rub vigorously. The printed image may rub off.

Repeat for all ovals. Allow the paste to dry. You may see small wrinkles develop in the wet paper. Summon all your willpower and do not try to eliminate wrinkles. The paper will shrink as it dries, and the wrinkles will disappear. Trying to get rid of the wrinkles will damage the paper.

4 *Planning plaster relief*

Set the hardware in place but do not attach it. Pencil plaster-relief patterns onto the dresser, avoiding the hardware. These patterns will be followed with the caulking gun.

Keep the lines simple, with large loops, avoiding intricate patterns and tight curves that can be difficult to follow with the large caulking gun. Straight lines are good for borders.

If your dresser has a mirror, mark where it sits so that the area can be avoided.

5 *Testing the caulking*

Cut off the tip of the plastic end of the caulking tube. Cut on an angle near the end, so that the hole in the tip is about ⅛ in. (3 mm) across. The tip can be recut later to a larger diameter, if desired. Insert a narrow sharp object, such as a piece of wire, into the tip and pierce the inside seal. (Some tips are removable for easy accessibility.) Load the tube of silicone caulking into the caulking gun and squeeze the trigger until caulking emerges from the tip.

On cardboard or a scrap piece of wood, do some test lines and squiggles to get a feel for the flow of the caulking. When applying caulking, drag the tip, creating contact between the caulking and the wood. No problem if you make a mistake. Scrape off the caulking while it is still damp and start again. Keep a rag handy on which to place the gun when you're pausing, since the caulking will continue to ooze.

Allow the caulking to dry. It will shrink as it dries. If the lines are too narrow and appear insignificant, recut the nozzle to a wider diameter.

6 *Caulking straight lines*

Remove the hardware from the drawer fronts. Do all straight lines first. Lay a yardstick along the line. Resting the tip of the nozzle against the dresser and the side of the nozzle against the wood, gently depress the trigger and make a line of caulking. At the end of the line, release the trigger and lift the gun off. Carefully remove the yardstick without touching the wet caulking. Let the caulking set.

The lines will not be perfect. They should be lumpy and somewhat uneven. A small point of caulking will be formed whenever the gun is lifted off, to be remedied later.

Finish caulking all straight lines.

7 *Caulking curves*

Caulking carefully around the pictures, cover the cut edge of the paper. Then, begin caulking along the curved lines. This job must be done freehand. Don't expect to follow the pencil lines exactly. They are only a guide.

As the caulking becomes dry to the touch, it is still wet inside. Using your fingers, press down any unwanted points. Allow the caulking to dry and harden.

8 *Painting*

Using a square-tipped artist's brush, paint around and over all the caulking details with the bone or sage green latex paint.

A fine-point artist's brush is useful for painting the caulking around the pictures.

Using a paint brush and a small roller, paint the rest of the dresser. Apply a second coat, if necessary, to achieve solid coverage.

9 *Antiquing*

To antique the dresser, use acrylic or latex paint in a similar yet much darker tone than the base coat. Use deep olive green for antiquing a sage green base coat, or burnt umber for a bone-colored base coat. Thin the paint to a watery consistency.

Brush the paint over a section of the caulking, working it into all details.

Allow the paint to pool in low spots. Wipe excess paint off high spots with a damp rag. Continue until all caulking has been antiqued. If desired, antique any trim or other details.

10 *Highlights*

To highlight the plaster-relief with gold, dip a brush into gold acrylic paint, wiping out the excess on a rag. Drag the brush lightly over the top ridges of the caulking, allowing paint to cling to the high areas.

Enrich color and protect the découpaged images and the paint job by varnishing the dresser with non-yellowing, water-based varnish. (See *Varnishing,* page 48.)

PATTERN FOR OVAL TEMPLATE

Wrapture

AN INGLORIOUS GROUP GOES GLAMOROUS, WRAPPED IN SPLENDID FABRICS

Pattern, texture, color. These chairs are at once
tactile, breathtaking, intriguing. The
scrunching and wrapping of the fabric
produces a potpourri of color and pattern,
turning butterflies and flowers into abstract art
with fantastic texture. The fabric's full pattern
is displayed on the seat cushion, coordinating
perfectly with the wrapping. Chair feet and
knobs are treated to humorously puffy covers.
Each seat is one of a kind, a serendipitous
mixture of color and pattern placement.
No two could ever be exactly the same.

Read This First

Small wrought iron tables or chairs, the rustier and more decrepit the better, are ideal for this treatment. The rust is covered with rust-coating spray paint. The damage is covered by the textured fabric. A bamboo chair can also be wrapped, although the job is somewhat more time-consuming because of the indigenous filigrees and fiddleheads. All chairs to be wrapped must be spray painted in a light color before wrapping. A dark color will show through light-colored fabric, giving it a dirty appearance. If you wish to apply this treatment to a table or desk, see *Material Pleasures* (page 68) and *Office Romance* (page 98) for information on covering a tabletop so that it will withstand wear.

Choose lightweight fabrics, which don't fray easily. These are easier to find in a dressmaker's fabric store than in an upholstery or a decorator's shop. Using a heavier cotton demands a more tailored approach, which is also shown. Tiny, repetitive patterns will look similar on the chair to how they appear on the bolt. Medium to large all-over prints make an interesting abstract pattern. Stripes will create sections of color. While the suggested quantity of fabric may seem excessive, it's difficult to assess the exact yardage needed for wrapping, plus cushions.

BEFORE

*Left, three wrought iron chairs. The rust damage could be covered with paint, but why not go for originality? **Right**, a bamboo chair painted deep brown and well worn (see finished chair, page 85). Repairing bamboo is practically impossible.*

MATERIALS

- screwdriver
- tape measure
- steel-wool soap pad
- packing tape or duct tape
- can of spray paint in a pale color that coordinates with the fabric (Choose rust-covering paint for wrought iron.)
- 2½ yd. (2.25 m) lightweight, patterned fabric, 54 in. (135 cm) wide, for a simple wrought iron chair (Purchase more fabric for intricate chairs.)
- scissors
- masking tape
- white carpenter's glue or craft glue
- scraps of terrycloth or similar fabric, 4 rubber bands
- *optional:* garden clippers (for cutting the cane of a bamboo seat)
- *optional:* small amount of coordinating paint for highlighting, artist's brush (step 2)
- *optional:* crochet hook
- *optional:* dressmaker's pins, iron-on interfacing, needle and thread, iron
- *optional:* fabric protector spray

I *Removing cushions*

Remove the seat cushion by turning the chair upside-down and unscrewing the screws. If the chair has a backrest, remove it too. Don't throw out either piece. The plywood inside the cushion is needed for recovering. Remove the old covering and foam and clean up the plywood. Measure and replace the plywood for the seat, if desired. But keep the formed plywood from the backrest. It is difficult to replace.

If your chair is bamboo, the seat may be woven into the chair with cane in one or two spots. Remove the seat by cutting the cane with garden clippers.

2 *Spray painting*

Wash the wrought iron chair with soap and water. Use a steel-wool soap pad to remove as much rust as possible. Rinse well and allow to dry thoroughly.

On a bamboo chair, glue down any broken cane. Wrap loose areas very tightly in packing tape or duct tape.

Spray paint the chair in a pale color similar to your fabric, following the directions on the can. Apply two coats if necessary.

When spraying a wrought iron chair, make sure all rust is completely covered. (See *Spray Painting,* page 44.)

Optional: If the chair has nice detail that you want to leave exposed, then, before wrapping, paint the area with a color to complement your fabric. Use acrylic or latex paint.

3 *Cutting fabric*

Cutting across the width of the fabric, cut twenty strips of fabric, 2 in. (5 cm) wide. Set aside fifteen strips. Cut five strips in half lengthwise to give you ten narrower ones. These are for fine filigree.

When using a heavy fabric, press a narrow hem on one edge, folding and ironing it toward the wrong side.

4 *Wrapping*

Start wrapping on the finest filigrees or spindles. The fine filigrees inevitably run to bigger ones that, when wrapped, will hide any loose fabric ends.

Cut and reserve some small pieces of masking tape. Dab glue at the starting point of a fine filigree (where it joins a larger one). Lay the end of a fabric strip onto the glue and tape it in place. Start wrapping. Bunch lightweight fabric and begin winding it tightly on a diagonal, covering any visible glue or tape. Overlap each previous edge of wrapped fabric.

With a heavier fabric, wrap the fabric flat, tight and even for a tailored look instead of bunching it as you wrap. Make sure the pressed edge overlaps the previous raw edge. Snip into the raw edge of the fabric, as needed, to work around obstacles. Should the chair have filigrees that end in points midair (very unusual), see step 5 for finishing the ends.

5 *Wrapping, continued*

At the end of each filigree, glue and tape the fabric down and cut the fabric. Leave

1 in. (2.5 cm) of excess, to be tucked under and covered later.

As you work, prevent the fabric from slipping by dabbing glue onto the wrought iron and wrapping over it. You can use dressmaker's pins to hold fabric in place. A crochet hook can be helpful for pulling fabric through tight spots.

Wrap the next group of filigrees, according to fatness. When passing the junctions of previously wrapped filigrees, tuck any excess fabric under, gluing and wrapping over it. Avoid leaving any gaps at junctions.

Continue wrapping all filigrees and spindles.

6 *Covering feet*

Before wrapping the chair legs, cover the feet. Cut four circles of fabric, 6 in. (15 cm) in diameter, and four circles of padding (terrycloth will do), 4 in. (10 cm) in diameter. Center the padding pieces on the wrong side of the fabric circles.

Place a circle under a foot of the chair, padding-side-up. Apply glue near the edge of the padding, draw up the edge of the circle, and wind a rubber band around the leg to bunch and secure the fabric circle. Repeat with the three remaining feet and fabric circles.

This technique can also be used to cover knobs or the ends of chair arms.

7 *Final wrapping*

Wrap the final (largest) sections, the legs, the rim of the seat and the back. Begin close to the feet, gluing and taping the end of the strip and tucking it under the raw edge. As you proceed, cover any loose ends.

8 *Covering fiddleheads*

To cover floral decorations on wrought iron or fiddleheads on a bamboo chair, first press iron-on interfacing onto the wrong side of a piece of fabric to prevent fraying.

Cut 2½ in. (6.25 cm) circles from the fabric, large enough to cover the fiddle-

heads completely in the style of a draw-string purse. Hold the circle to the fiddlehead. Then cut into the side of the circle, fitting the cut around the area where the fiddlehead joins the chair.

Remove the circle of fabric. Beginning and ending at the cut, sew running stitches near the edge and gather slightly. Place the circle onto the fiddlehead and gather tightly so that the circle is snugly closed.

Optional: Spray with fabric protector.

9 *Cushions*

Cover any seat cushions or backrest cushions and attach to the chair. (For more about cushion covers, see *Seating,* page 110.)

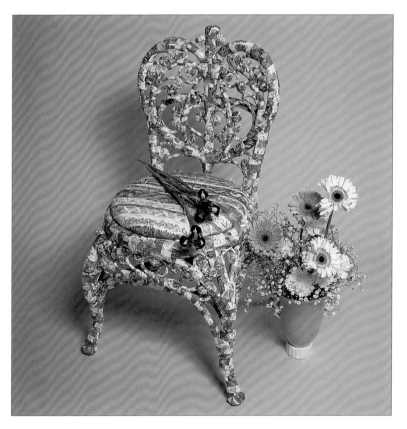

Shown here, the finished results of wrapping a bamboo chair – with all its attendant filigree and frippery – in a heavy cotton using a tailored approach.

Posterity

PLAYFUL, HISTORIC, ROMANTIC — POSTERS ADD MOOD AND DRAMA

Larger-than-life results start with a dramatic sense of scale.
An oversized poster, laminated to a dresser front, illustrates this concept
beautifully. Art posters capture any mood imaginable. Choose from
masters like Leonardo da Vinci or Rembrandt for rich sepia tones with warm
light. Draw on Miro, Mondrian or Picasso for a splash of color. Or look to
the ever-favorite impressionists for romance. The choices are unlimited.
Add background paint and detail, and watch your own masterpiece
fall into place with ease.

Floral Arrangements

TWIN BENTWOOD ARMCHAIRS ARE
ROMANCED WITH PAINT AND FABRIC

A splash of fresh flowers on a crisp white cotton background is the perfect foil for glossy white lacquer. Mixing texture, color and pattern creates dramatic change for any worn-out furniture, especially when the original is dark and dreary. Painting the fabric's design onto the seat of the chair moves the treatment from predictable to original, adding an artist's touch while echoing the fabric's design and colors. Thoroughly modern gathered halters create both a cover-up and new interest, a unique approach to a slipcover.

Read This First

These chairs are unusual because the backs were broken, while the seats, which were in perfect condition, were covered with bulky cushions. If your chair has a broken cane seat and a good back, reverse the treatment by painting the back and adding a fabric-covered cushion to the seat. If both the back and the cane seat are broken, make a halter and a cushion. (See *Seating*, page 110, for more about cushions.)

This treatment is accomplished in three phases. First, the chairs are spray painted. Then a portion of the fabric design is traced and painted on the seats. For ease of copying, choose a fabric with a large, uncomplicated pattern that looks brush painted. Finally, the backs are covered with gathered halters. The halters require only basic sewing. Halters are the perfect solution for a chair with a broken cane or spindle back.

BEFORE

Tweed cushions compromise the elegant lines of a pair of bentwood chairs. Damaged finish and broken backs demand an imaginative renovation.

MATERIALS

- can of acrylic spray paint, gloss finish, in an appropriate color
- dropsheet
- fabric (To determine yardage, see step 5.)
- tubes of acrylics to match colors in fabric, artist's brushes
- access to photocopier, or tracing paper and pencil
- scissors for cutting fabric and canvas
- piece of canvas to fit chair back (To determine size, see step 4.)
- stapler and ¼ in. (.5 cm) staples
- sewing machine with thread to match fabric, or needle and thread; dressmaker's pins
- white carpenter's glue, small brass nails, small hammer
- hot-glue gun
- iron
- *optional:* heavy-duty scissors or garden clippers, chisel, wood filler, fine sandpaper (220 grade)
- *optional:* tape measure, power drill, two small knobs
- *optional:* shirring tape

1 *Removing cane*

Remove the broken cane. Cut it away with heavy-duty scissors or garden clippers.

Then remove the stubble by cutting it off level with the wood, laying a chisel against the base and tapping it with a small hammer.

Fill any holes with wood filler and allow to dry. Sand smooth with fine sandpaper.

2 *Preparation and painting*

Optional: If your chair has round shoulders, create physical borders for the halter. Measure an equal distance both sides of center and drill holes for two knobs. Test that the knobs fit. Then remove them and set them aside.

Place the chair on a dropsheet and spray paint the chair. (See *Spray Painting,* page 44.)

3 *Painting the seat*

If the cane seat is in good condition, paint it as follows. Isolate an area of the fabric's design that will fit onto the seat of the chair. Photocopy or trace this area onto paper. Cut out elements of the design. Lay the cut-outs onto the seat and trace around them with a pencil. Using artist's brushes and the acrylics, follow the fabric as a color guide. Paint the shapes. Allow to dry.

If the cane is in poor condition, create a cushion. (See *Seating,* page 110.)

4 *Halter liner*

Without a canvas reinforcement, the finished halter will not support the weight of a seated person. Measure the height of the backrest and add 6 in (15 cm). Cut a piece of canvas to this length and to a width 2 in. (5 cm) narrower than the halter will be (step 5). Serge or glue along the sides to prevent fraying. Allow the glue to dry. Center the canvas onto the front side of the chair back. Wrap the end of the canvas around the bottom rail and staple the canvas to the rail. Pull the canvas very tightly around the top rail. Staple it securely in place.

5 *Sewing the halter*

Cut the halter fabric as follows. Measure the width of the halter. Cut fabric one-and-one-half times to twice the width. To determine the length of the fabric, measure the height of the backrest. Double the measurement and add 6 in. (15 cm) for finishing. Cut the fabric to this length.

To hem both sides, fold the side edges under, ½ in. (1.25 cm) to the wrong side. Repeat. Press, then sew close to the inside fold. Do not hem the ends.

Measure the length of the fabric and

mark the center. Gather across the fabric at the mark, either by sewing shirring tape to the wrong side or by sewing large stitches.

6 *Positioning the halter*

If using the knobs, attach them now through the drilled holes. Position the fabric with the gathering between the knobs, adjusting the gathers to fit.

Determine if the fabric has a pattern that runs in one direction, such as vines climbing a trellis. The fabric's design should run up on the front of the backrest. Center the gathers along the bentwood back, gluing and/or nailing the fabric in place with small brass nails. Cover the heads of the nails with the gathers.

7 *Attaching the halter*

Turn the chair upside-down, so that you are working with the fabric on the back of the chair back. Pull the halter fabric snugly to the center of the bottom rung, marking it with pins. Sew a running stitch along the pin line for gathering. Cut away excess fabric ½ in. (1.25 cm) outside the pin line. Gather the stitching.

Centering the gathers onto the bottom rung, use the hot-glue gun to glue the gathers to the bottom rung, pulling the fabric taut. *Be careful not to burn your fingers, especially if you are not experienced with a glue gun.* The glue becomes hot enough to cause deep burns, and the glue sticks and keeps burning.

Stand the chair up. Measure and cut the front fabric as you did for the back, adding a 1 in. (2.5 cm) hem. Flip the front fabric over and iron the 1 in. (2.5 cm) hem to the wrong side. Sew and gather along the crease of the hem.

Pull the fabric taut and hot glue the gathered edge along the center of the bottom rail, covering the raw edge.

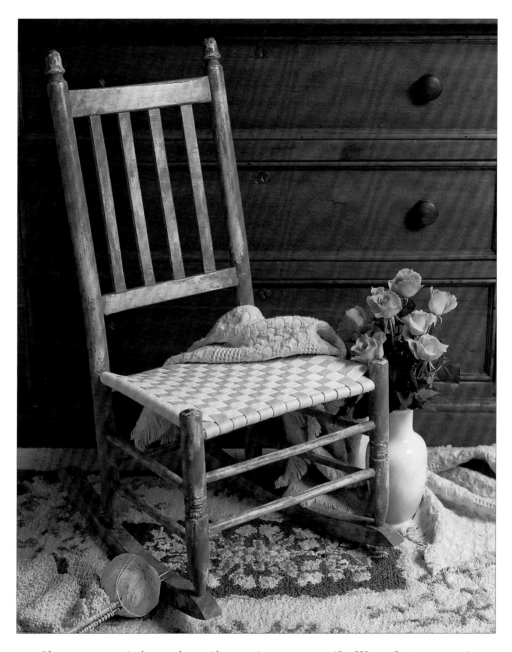

If your cane seat is damaged, consider weaving a new one. (See Woven Seat, page 119.)

Office Romance

FROM ORDINARY TO STUNNING — A DESK IS CLAD WITH GLORIOUS FABRIC

Covering a piece of furniture with fabric is easier than the elegant results would have you believe. Unusual, daring, breathtaking — a desk or dresser completely covered in rich, tactile fabric has it all and more. Decorator fabric shops offer an infinite choice of patterns and color combinations, allowing complete customizing of a desk or dresser. The intrinsically romantic and delicate properties of the fabric are preserved and protected with a coating of crystal clear varnish.

Read This First

If your fabric is narrower than the combined front and sides of the desk or dresser, sew two widths of fabric together matching the pattern, and press the seam open. If the fabric isn't sewn, there will be an obvious join on the front of the unit. The desk or dresser you choose should be very simple, without lumpy trims or decorations. It should have drawers with overhanging fronts, not the type that are set in. Wrapping fabric onto the sides of set-in drawers will cause the drawers to bind; that is, if they'll even fit back into their slots.

The best fabrics for this job are decorator fabrics in stable weaves, not knits – neither too heavy nor lightweight, and without a nap (such as velvet or corduroy would have). Stripes and intricate patterns can create problems when matching the pattern for a stack of drawers. Best bets are large, somewhat random patterns or tiny repetitive patterns such as polka dots. Consider mixes. Many companies print fabrics in coordinating patterns of small and large prints in the same colors. These can be used in a complementary way. Cover the background with the small print, and the drawers and top with the large print.

MATERIALS

- screwdriver
- 3 yd. (3 m) decorator fabric, 54 to 60 in. (135 to 150 cm) wide (quantity may vary according to size of furniture)
- ruler and pencil
- scissors
- cellulose-based wallpaper paste
- plastic dropsheet
- large, soft paint brush
- household sponge
- X-acto knife
- dressmaker's pins
- quart (litre) non-yellowing, water-based varnish
- fine sandpaper (220 grade), tack cloth
- *optional:* quart (litre) each: high-adhesion, water-based primer; white latex paint (step 1)
- *optional:* painting tools – paint brush, small roller, roller tray
- *optional:* staple gun and staples
- *optional:* access to photocopier
- *optional:* hot-glue gun or carpenter's glue

BEFORE

A 1970s-vintage student desk with a melamine top. The flat, flush-fit drawers and lack of detail make it ideal for covering with fabric.

1 *Preparation*

If possible, remove the desktop by taking out all drawers and turning the desk upside-down. (Recruit help if the desk is heavy.) Unscrew all screws that hold the top in place.

Remove all hardware and sand any lumps or bumps off the surface of the desk. Even very small bumps will pucker the fabric.

If the fabric has areas that are pale in tone, variations in the color of the desk will show through the fabric. To avoid this problem, use a water-based primer to paint any areas that are not pure white, covering stains and any printed decorations. If the imperfections show through the primer at all, recoat the areas with white paint. If the finish on the desk is a color other than white, prime the desk and paint it white. (Refer to *Painting Basics,* page 34.) Allow to dry.

2 *Cutting fabric*

Hold the fabric against the front of the desk, measuring and marking the height plus a 2 in. (5 cm) allowance for both the top and the bottom. If the design on the fabric is directional (vines climbing a trellis, for example), position the fabric right-way-up. Cut straight across the fabric.

Check that the fabric is wide enough to cover the front (where the drawers go) and two adjoining sides. (See *Read This First,* previous page.)

3 *Wallpaper paste*

Following the manufacturer's instructions, mix a small bucket or bowl of the wallpaper paste.

Lay the cut piece of fabric wrong-side-up on a plastic dropsheet. Using the large, soft paint brush, spread an even layer of paste over the fabric, saturating it.

4 *Fitting fabric to the desk front*

Tip the desk onto its back (drawers removed) and drape the pasted fabric over the body of the desk. The fabric should cover the front where the drawers belong, the outer side of the desk, and the adjacent side of the knee hole, with excess to wrap onto the back. Smooth the fabric with a moist sponge, eliminating air pockets and keeping the fabric damp. The principle of this technique is to keep surfaces smooth where they will be seen, and cut edges wrapped and pasted where they will not be seen.

Finish the bottom edges of the desk by pasting and smoothing the excess fabric and wrapping it to the inside of the desk.

This desk has a curvy bottom edge along the front. To make the fabric conform, multiple cuts were made along the edge. Then the fabric was smoothed and pasted to the underside.

5 *Finishing drawer openings*

Using a sharp X-acto knife, cut a small X in the center of a drawer opening. Using scissors, expand the X, cutting to the corners of the opening.

Trim the four V-shapes of fabric and smooth them over the edges, wrapping them to the inside of the desk.

Repeat for all drawer openings. If sections begin to dry, add more paste as needed and keep the fabric moist with a damp sponge.

6 *Fitting fabric, continued*

Stand the desk upright. Trim the fabric to a neat overlap along the top and back edges of the desk. Wrap it over the edge to the inside, and paste it down.

Keep corners neat by cutting away excess fabric, then folding and pasting in place. Corners that will not be seen can be stapled.

Check over the fabric, making sure it is pasted securely in place with no loose edges or air pockets.

Continue pasting fabric to the rest of the desk, matching the pattern as you go. Where fabric joins, fold the edge under, like a narrow seam, to avoid a raw edge. Allow the paste to dry. As it dries, check that it doesn't lift. If lifting occurs, wet the fabric well with a sponge dipped in paste and smooth it down.

7 *Cutting for drawer fronts*

Because of the necessary wraparounds on each drawer front, the repeats on your fabric must be cut from three separate, repeat areas of fabric to match the pattern of the fabric already laminated to the desk.

Place the top drawer in position. Cut a generous piece of fabric, larger than the drawer front, that matches the section of fabric pattern already laminated to the body of the desk.

Drape the fabric over the drawer front, matching the pattern to the body of the desk. With the fabric in place, mark the four corners of the drawer front with pins.

Remove the fabric with the pins in place and trim some of the excess fabric away, leaving at least 1 in. (2.5 cm) as an overlap. Apply paste to the fabric.

8 *Laminating drawer fronts*

Drape the fabric onto the drawer front, placing the marker pins at the corners. Check that the drawer and the fabric are both right-way-up. Trim the excess fabric again, leaving enough to wrap over onto the inside edge of the drawer. Remove the pins.

To create a neat corner, clip the fabric to the corner of the drawer front. Smooth one side under, pasting it to the inside edge.

Then fold the point of the second side under. Smooth this side onto the inside edge.

9 *Covering the desktop*

Cut fabric for the top as follows. Check that the fabric pattern matches the body of the desk and that it runs in the right direction, from front to back. Check also that there is enough overlap onto the wrong side for raw edges to be hidden when the top is reattached to the body. If the fabric isn't wide enough, try running the pattern lengthwise. Some large patterns are acceptable either way. As an alternative, consider painting the desktop a coordinating color. You could also photocopy the pattern of the fabric and

découpage it on the top at random. (See *Prints Charming,* page 56.) Paste the fabric to the desktop, folding and trimming to make neat corners. Allow to dry.

As the drawer fronts dry, check that the overlap onto the inside edge is stuck down. If it lifts, glue it with a hot-glue gun or carpenter's glue. *If using a glue gun, be careful not to burn your fingers.* The glue becomes hot enough to cause deep burns, and it sticks and keeps burning.

10 *Varnishing*

When the paste is thoroughly dry, all fabric areas must be varnished for protection. Apply a coat of non-yellowing, water-based varnish to all fabric surfaces. Allow the varnish to dry completely. Apply a second coat of varnish to all fabric surfaces. Allow to dry.

Using a fine sandpaper, very lightly sand the varnished surfaces. Don't be alarmed by a cloudy effect on the fabric's colors. Wipe all residue and dust from the sanding with a tack cloth. Varnish again. If the fabric is still porous, repeat the sanding and varnishing.

Reattach the desktop and the hardware.

Botanical Design

GRAPEVINES AND SOPHISTICATED COLOR
PRODUCE A CRAFTED CABINET

Nothing creates style quite like the melding of a rich palette with the textures
and forms of nature. Earthy olive green paint and gray-stained natural wood
complement the controlled chaos of grapevines artfully arranged over
laminated, parchment-thin golden grape leaves. The marriage of city
and country flavors makes this armoire adaptable to virtually
any room in either environment.

Read This First

Part of the pleasure of finishing this piece of furniture is the experience of finding and collecting leaves and vines. If grapevines are not available in your area, collect leaves that are a suitable shape and buy the vines from a florist or craft shop. Leaves must be pressed and dried for at least two weeks. If you do collect your own vines, do it in the summer or fall when the vines are pliable. Wear boots, long pants, and gloves – and watch out for poison ivy. Pull out good long lengths, the thicker the stem, the better. As you pull the vine down, wind and tie it into a coil, small enough to fit into a sink or laundry tub since the vines will later need soaking to rejuvenate them.

Collect leaves in the summer, if possible. By fall, grape leaves tend to be very fragile and thin. And fall colors aren't necessary because the leaves tend to change from green to a golden green-brown as they dry. While the leaves are drying, stain the cabinet's trim. Prime and paint the body with a base coat. If your armoire has a plastic laminate finish, use melamine paint for the base coat. (See *Melamine Paint,* page 27.)

BEFORE

An inexpensive unpainted wardrobe made of pine with very thin mahogany board panels can become a one-of-a-kind horticultural presence. All it needs are the right touches.

MATERIALS

- 2 dozen grape leaves
- scissors and a thick phone book
- 20 to 30 yd. (20 to 30 m) grapevines (allows for two vines on each side and two on the front, plus a generous portion for top arrangement)
- fine sandpaper (220 grade)
- pale- to medium-gray stain
- rag
- fine-point artist's brush
- easy-release painter's tape
- quart (litre) high-adhesion, water-based primer
- quart (litre) eggshell finish latex paint, deep olive green
- painting tools: paint brush, small roller, roller tray
- quart (litre) non-yellowing, water-based varnish
- paper towels
- carpet staples, small hammer
- garden clippers
- small quantity cellulose-based wallpaper paste

1 *Leaves*

Snip stems off the leaves and press them in a phone book. Leave about twenty pages between each page of leaves. Allow leaves to dry for at least two weeks.

2 *Vines*

Place a coil of vines in a bucket or sink and cover them with water. Soak the vines while the cabinet is being painted or for two hours.

3 *Staining trim*

Stain can be applied only to raw wood. (See *Staining Wood,* page 46.) Using fine sandpaper, lightly sand all areas that will be stained.

Remove doors and hardware. Place the doors on a tabletop and work on them while you work on the cabinet.

Stir the stain thoroughly. Using the artist's brush, apply stain along recessed trim or other hard-to-reach areas.

Using a rag or a paint brush, apply stain to the trim. Allow to dry.

4 *Painting panels*

Mask off all stained trim. Prime the panels and paint them with the deep olive green paint. (See *Painting Basics,* page 34.) Allow to dry.

Apply one coat of non-yellowing, water-based varnish to the stained areas of the armoire. Allow to dry, then repeat. Varnish can also be applied over the paint if desired. (See *Varnishing,* page 48.)

5 *Attaching vines*

Unwind the vines and pat them dry with paper towels. When the armoire is thoroughly dry, lay it on its side. (If the armoire is heavy, recruit a helper.) Starting at the bottom of the armoire, arrange the vines onto the uppermost side.

Starting at the bottom edge of the armoire, hammer carpet staples into the trim, anchoring the vine. Use as many staples as necessary to keep the vine reasonably close to the surface of the armoire.

Using garden clippers, cut the vine cleanly at the bottom edge of the armoire. Continue stapling the vine in place on the full side of the armoire. Don't cut off any excess vine at the top of the armoire.

Stand the armoire up (get help if needed) and arrange any trailing vines from the side along the top edge, stapling them in place. Don't allow them to hang in the door space. Otherwise, the door won't shut. Staple vines to the other side of the armoire and work any trailing vines into the top arrangement. Staple vines to the door panels, keeping them within the trim and working from a bottom corner to the opposite top corner.

6 Laminating leaves

Follow the instructions on the package of wallpaper paste to mix a small quantity.

Coat both sides of a leaf with the paste, leaving no dry spots.

Lay the leaf onto the surface of the armoire, aligning it with the vine. Smooth it from the center, eliminating any air pockets. Continue, pasting leaves on both sides of the armoire. The leaves may become wrinkly. The wrinkles will disappear as the leaves dry and shrink. Avoid trying to stretch the leaves flat. You will only damage the leaves.

7 Doors

Reattach the doors. Laminate leaves onto the doors. Allow both the vines and the leaves to dry.

8 Varnishing

Brush two coats of varnish over the leaves to protect them.

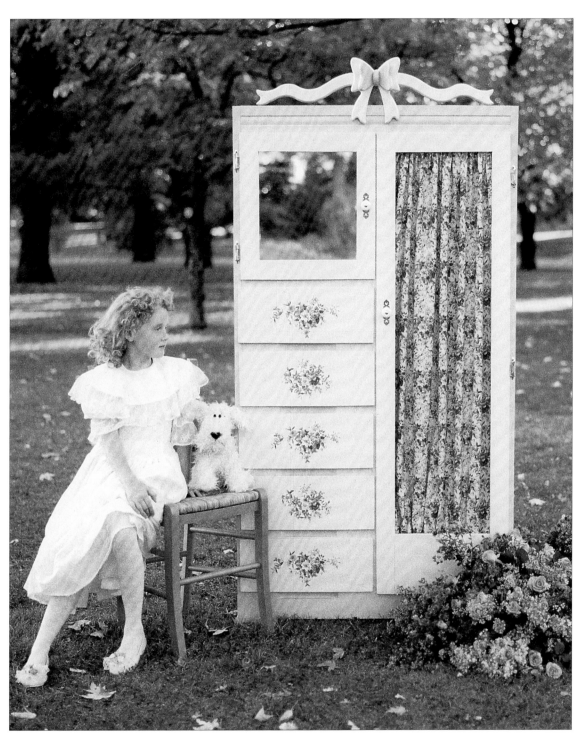

Old wardrobes are often missing glass or mirror from their doors. They can benefit from an attractive curtain treatment. (See page 60.) Choose a print that complements the leaf treatment.

Seating

SITTING PRETTY WITH PROFESSIONALLY CRAFTED CUSHIONS AND SEATS

The seat of a chair is more than a place to park. Chair seats and cushions offer a design opportunity to add texture, color and pattern with fabric — along with a higher degree of comfort. Try to find an upholstery supplier that sells upholsterer's-quality high-density foam, batting, and dust-cover cloth. Dust-cover cloth is the non-fraying fabric that goes under the seat to cover raw edges and bare plywood. If you can, take along the plywood base from the old cushion as a pattern, and have the foam pieces cut to fit.

Following are instructions for a basic seat cushion, a piped seat cushion, and a woven webbing seat, along with two treatments for backrest cushions — tailored and shirred. Only the piped cushion requires sewing.

Above, the chair on the left
has a basic seat cushion and a
shirred backrest cushion. The
chair on the right has a piped
seat cushion. *Left,* both chairs
have basic seat cushions and
tailored backrest cushions.

Basic Seat Cushion

Read This First

This seat cushion is the type that looks like a large soft cookie. Use this treatment primarily on round chair seats. Square seats tend to look better with a straight-sided or piped cushion. Choose the thickness of the foam, between one and two inches (2.5 to 5 cm), depending on the style of the chair. If the thicker foam will obscure detailing or be ungainly in height, choose a thinner foam. It will look better, but the trade-off will be a harder chair and slightly less comfort for those sitting on it. Buy plywood that is good one side. This means that one side has a smooth finish, while the other is knotty and rough. The good side of the plywood will be positioned down on the seat. (Good both sides, which is much more expensive, is not necessary.)

MATERIALS

- plywood, ½ in. (1.25 cm) thick, good one side, cut to fit the seat of the chair
- high-density upholstery foam, 1 to 2 in (2.5 to 5 cm) thick, cut to fit plywood
- fabric, 8 in. (20 cm) larger than the plywood both in length and in width
- iron
- ruler and marker
- scissors
- batting, 6 in. (15 cm) larger than the plywood both in length and in width
- stapler and ⅜ in. (1 cm) staples
- non-fraying upholstery dust-cover cloth (enough to cover the plywood)
- screws (to reattach cushion to chair), screwdriver
- *optional:* jigsaw
- *optional:* spray glue; scrap paper or dropsheet
- *optional:* lining (step 5)

1 Getting started

Remove the fabric and foam from the underlying plywood. Clean the plywood as thoroughly as possible, removing any mold and staples.

If the old plywood is beyond salvation, have a new piece cut or cut one yourself with a jigsaw. The new plywood should be ½ in. (1.25 cm) thick, good one side.

Have a piece of high-density upholstery foam cut to match the size and shape of the plywood.

2 Cutting fabric

Iron the fabric.

Lay the foam or the plywood onto the wrong side of the fabric. Measure and mark the fabric 4 in. (10 cm) from the edge of the foam. Do this at regular intervals around the perimeter of the foam. Join the marks to make a continuous solid line.

Cut along the line.

3 Laminating foam to plywood

Optional: Gluing the foam to the plywood can reduce slippage. Lay down some scrap paper or a dropsheet and place the foam onto it. Check the directions on the spray-glue label for making a permanent bond. Spray the foam with glue.

Lay the rough side of the plywood on the gluey foam, centering it.

4 Batting

Lay the plywood/foam onto the batting. Lift the batting up, against the side of the foam, marking the batting at the top edge of the foam. Do this all the around the foam.

Cut the batting along the marked line.

Optional: With the plywood/foam centered on the circle of batting, foam-side-down, spray-glue a section of the overhanging batting. Fold the glued section up onto the foam. Repeat until the batting is glued to the perimeter of the foam.

5 *Stapling*

If the cushion fabric is lightweight, cut a lining from a woven material such as broadcloth. Lay the fabric face-down, with the lining on top.

Position the plywood/foam/batting sandwich, batting-side-down, onto the center of the fabric. Gently but firmly, pull and staple the fabric to the plywood in four places, equal distances apart.

Gently but firmly, pull and staple the fabric to the plywood between each of the four staples, keeping the pressure even.

Gently but firmly, pull and staple the fabric to the plywood between each of the eight staples, keeping the pressure even.

Gently but firmly, pull and staple the fabric to the plywood between the staples. Continue until the fabric is stapled evenly all around.

6 *Finishing*

Cut a circle of dust-cover cloth slightly larger than the circle of staples, but smaller than the bottom of the cushion. Staple it to the bottom of the cushion, starting with four equidistant staples. Then staple between them, as you did to staple the cushion fabric, until the full perimeter is stapled.

Reattach the cushion to the chair by screwing appropriately sized screws into the seat frame and the plywood of the cushion. Work from underneath the seat.

Piped Seat Cushion

Read This First

Making a piped seat cushion takes some planning and sewing ability, although the sewing is actually basic and straightforward. The piping gives the cushion an elegant, crisp finish. Piping is available in braids or wovens, and it comes in a wide range of colors, prints and finishes, from shiny to matte. Choose a piping that will coordinate with the fabric, yet stand out enough to accentuate the tailored edge. If you have never sewn piping with a piping foot on your sewing machine, here's a chance to try it and see how professional the results are. The sewing goes faster and is easier if a piping foot is used. It keeps the piping on track and the sewing uniform. If a piping foot is not available, use a zipper foot.

MATERIALS

- plywood, ½ in. (1.25 cm) thick, good one side, cut to fit the seat of the chair
- high-density upholstery foam, 2 in. (5 cm) thick, cut to match the plywood
- paper, pencil, ruler
- fabric, approx. ½ yd. (.5 m) for each cushion
- scissors
- piping (measure perimeter of cushion and add 6 in. (15 cm))
- dressmaker's pins
- sewing machine with piping foot
- thread to match fabric
- batting, 6 in. (15 cm) larger than the plywood both in length and in width
- stapler and ⅜ in. (1 cm) staples
- non-fraying upholstery dust-cover cloth (enough to cover the plywood)
- screws (to reattach cushion to chair), screwdriver
- *optional:* jigsaw
- *optional:* zipper foot
- *optional:* spray glue; scrap paper or drop-sheet

1 *Getting started*

Remove the fabric and foam from the underlying plywood. Clean the plywood as thoroughly as possible, removing any mold and staples.

If the old plywood is beyond repair, have a new piece cut or cut one yourself with a jigsaw. The new plywood should be ½ in. (1.25 cm) thick, good one side.

Have a piece of high-density upholstery foam, 2 in. (5 cm) thick, professionally cut to match the size and shape of the plywood.

2 *Drafting a pattern*

Make a pattern for the top of the cushion cover. Lay the plywood onto paper and trace closely around it. Using a ruler, measure and mark a ½ in. (1.25 cm) seam allowance from the plywood edge all around the perimeter. Then join the marks to create a cutting line.

3 *Cutting fabric*

Cut out the pattern and lay it onto the fabric, centering it carefully onto the fabric's design. If the design printed on the fabric is directional (vines climbing a trellis, for example), it should run from the front of the cushion "up" to the back.

On fabric with a geometric pattern, the placement should match for all cushions. Pin the pattern in place and cut out the fabric for all cushions.

For the sides of the cushion cover, cut strips of fabric, 6 in. (15 cm) wide, across the width of the fabric. Cut the strips to match up with the fabric design of the cushion tops, taking into consideration the width of seam allowances. Usually, one width of fabric will circle one cushion.

4 *Sewing*

Starting at the center-back of the cushion top, pin piping on the right side of the fabric, matching the raw edge of the piping to the cut edge of the fabric. Check that the piping has a ½ in. (1.25 cm) seam allowance. If not, compensate. Pin well. At corners, clip into the seam allowance of the piping, allowing it to bend. At the start and the end, allow 2 in. (5 cm) extra piping, laying the ends across the seam allowance.

Attach the piping foot to the sewing machine. With matching thread, begin at the center-back and sew the piping in place, ½ in. (1.25 cm) from the cut edge.

Lay a cut strip of fabric onto the piped edge of the cushion, with right sides together, matching the pattern along the front edge of the cushion. The ends of the strip should join at the center back. Pin the strip to the cushion top, starting at the center-front and working out, until the strip is pinned to the full perimeter of the cushion top. Clip the seam allowance of the strip at corners, if necessary. If the strip is too short, sew an additional section to the strip.

With the piping foot still in place, sew the strip tightly against the piping. Join the ends of the strip. Turn the cushion cover right-side-out and inspect the seam. Resew any gaps.

5 *Batting*

Using the foam as a guide, cut a piece of batting 3 in. (7.5 cm) larger all around (or measure and cut batting as shown on page 156, step 4). Lay the foam onto the plywood and the batting onto the foam. Notch the corners, so they dovetail when bent down over the sides of foam.

Optional: Gluing the foam to the plywood and the batting to the foam can reduce slippage. (See *Basic Seat Cushion*, steps 3 and 4, page 113.)

   If you opt not to glue the plywood and the batting to the foam, lay the foam onto the rough side of the plywood and center the batting over the foam.

Slip the piped cushion top over the batting.

6 *Stapling*

Turn the cushion upside-down. At the center of each side, gently but firmly pull the fabric to the back of the cushion and staple in place.

Continue, adding staples equally to all sides, keeping the tension even. Don't staple one full side before going on to the next. This will cause uneven tension and ripples.

Finish corners by stapling the center of the corner, then folding and stapling the excess down, like a fan, on both sides. Do several small folds to avoid puckering.

7 *Finishing*

Cut a piece of dust-cover cloth to fit the bottom of the cushion. It should cover the staples but be within the edge of the cushion. Staple it in place with one staple centered on each side. Work out from these staples, stapling all around the edge.

Reattach the cushion to the chair by screwing in appropriately sized screws from the bottom of the seat.

Woven Seat

Read This First

This technique is for replacing a worn-out webbing or split-cane seat. The seat must have the necessary dowel-like four rungs: front, back and sides. Purchase webbing at an upholstery supply store or buy wicking for oil lamps. The wicking shown here was bought at a hardware store in a 25 yard (23 m) roll for a surprisingly modest price. The wicking is a flatly woven natural cotton of a pleasing width. But why stop here? Many cast-off items can be used to great effect. Layers of ribbon, bunched yarn, or ends of trims can be used. Torn rags, tied end to end, could give a folksy, rag-rug feeling to a seat. Once started, stick to this project until finished (it only takes a few hours), so you won't lose track of the weaving.

MATERIALS

- approx. 20 yd. (20 m) wicking (the type used for oil lamps) or webbing about 1 in. (2.5 cm) wide (amount required can vary, depending on size of chair seat)
- stiff cardboard, 3 x 6 in. (7.5 x 15 cm)
- ruler and marker
- stir stick or other narrow stick, to fit the width of the seat
- white carpenter's glue and tape, or stapler and ¼ in. (.5 cm) staples
- *optional:* needle and thread for sewing webbing ends

1 *Getting started*

Cut a rectangle of stiff cardboard, about 3 x 6 in. (7.5 x 15 cm). Wrap the webbing around the length of the cardboard from end to end to make a shuttle. Don't cut the webbing.

Mark the center points on the front and back rungs of the seat. The markings will help you keep the weaving straight, especially if the rungs are different lengths.

2 *The first pass*

Stand in front, facing the chair. Begin on the left side. Glue and tape (or staple) the webbing to the left-side rung. (Glue, tape and staples will be hidden by the weaving.)

Slip the shuttle under the back rung, then bring it up and over the back rung and toward the front, keeping the webbing flat.

Bring the shuttle forward, passing over the front rung, then under the chair seat to the back, and over the back rung again.

Keep the webbing even, neat and tight.

Continue until the full seat is covered, ending on top at the front right corner.

3 *Weaving*

Slip the shuttle under the seat to the back right. Bring it up, over the back rung, then under the right-side rung.

Weave the first row by bringing the shuttle over the right rung. Pass it *over the first strip* of webbing and under the second. Continue this over-under motion across the full width.

Using a ruler (or stir stick, as shown here), prop up the alternating strips under which you will pass. When you finish a row, remove the stick and reposition it for the next row. This will make the weaving easier and help you to avoid errors.

Turn the chair upside-down and weave across the back of the seat, as you did for the front.

Turn the chair right-side-up again. Reposition the ruler or stick. Weave the second row by bringing the shuttle up over the right-side rung. Pass the shuttle *under the first strip* and over the second. Then continue across the full width of the seat.

4 *Weaving, continued*

Continue in this manner, alternating the over-under weaving pattern. Stop to check the pattern occasionally. Keep the weaving tight by pushing it together with the tip of the ruler or stick.

About halfway through the weaving, the shuttle may not fit through between the webbing. Take the webbing off the shuttle and pull it through in a loosely gathered bunch.

If the webbing isn't long enough and you need to join it, sew the ends together on the underside of the seat and tuck in any loose ends.

5 *Finishing*

Weave to the last row.

On the underside, weave halfway across the last row. Then cut the webbing and glue (or sew) the end down, tucking away any excess.

Backrest Cushions

Read This First

The decision to have a tailored or a shirred cushion on the seat's backrest is based on the style of the chair. A tailored cushion doesn't stand out. It is an integral part of the design of the chair. A shirred cushion, in contrast, commands attention. It makes a statement, giving the chair a showy, fashion-conscious sensibility. A tailored backrest cushion can be made from any type of fabric. A shirred backrest should be made from lightweight, finely woven fabric. The backrest can be finished decoratively with braid trim on the back side to hide staples, or by carefully gluing the finishing panel in place for a clean, crisp look.

MATERIALS

- plywood, ½ in. (1.25 cm) thick, good one side, to fit chair back (If the backrest is curved, reserve plywood from existing cushion.)
- high-density upholstery foam, 1 in. (2.5 cm) thick, cut to match the shape of the plywood
- fabric (To determine yardage, see step 2.)
- tape measure
- batting, 4 in. (10 cm) larger than the plywood both in length and in width
- stapler and ⅜ in. (1 cm) staples
- *for shirred cushion:* needle and thread
- hot-glue gun
- *for trimmed back:* 2 yd. (2 m) braid trim, 2 small pieces of tape
- dressmaker's pins
- screws (to reattach seat to chair), screwdriver
- small amount of paint to match fabric (for heads of screws)
- utility knife or X-acto knife
- *optional:* spray glue; scrap paper or dropsheet

1 *Getting started*

For all cushions: Remove the fabric and foam from the underlying plywood. Clean the plywood as thoroughly as possible, removing any mold and staples.

Have a piece of high-density upholstery foam, 1 in. (2.5 cm) thick, cut to match the size and shape of the plywood. Although it is best to have the foam professionally cut, foam this thin can be cut with scissors.

2 *Cutting fabric*

For tailored cushions: Lay the foam (or the plywood) onto the wrong side of the fabric. If the design printed on the fabric is directional (vines climbing a wall, for example), it should run up, from bottom of backrest to top. Measure and mark a cutting line 3 in. (7.5 cm) from the foam. Do this around the full perimeter. Cut along the line.

For shirred cushions: Measure the deepest section of the plywood backrest. Add 5 in. (12.5 cm). Cut fabric to this depth and to double the width of the backrest. Set the fabric aside.

For all cushions: Cut a piece of fabric 1 in. (2.5 cm) larger on all sides than the foam. This will be used to cover the back of the backrest cushion. If the design printed on the fabric is directional (vines climbing a wall, for example), it should run up, from bottom of backrest to top. Set the fabric aside.

3 *Cutting batting, gluing foam*

For all cushions: Cut batting 1½ in. (4 cm) larger on all sides than the foam. Notch the corners of the batting so that they dovetail when the batting is folded over the sides of the foam. Set the batting aside.

Optional: Gluing the foam to the plywood can reduce slippage. Lay down some scrap paper or a dropsheet and place the foam onto it. Check the directions on the spray-glue label for making a permanent bond. Spray the foam with glue.

Lay the gluey side of the foam onto the front side of the plywood.

4 *Gluing batting*

For all cushions. Optional: Lay the plywood and foam, foam-side-down, onto the batting. Using the spray glue, spray a section of the overhanging batting and fold the glued section up onto the side of the foam and plywood. Repeat until the batting is glued to the edges of the foam all the way around.

5 *Shirring*

For shirred cushions: By machine or by hand, sew along the top and bottom edges of the fabric and gather to the width of the seat back, plus 5 in. (12.5 cm).

6 *Stapling*

For tailored cushions: Lay the fabric face-down. Center the plywood/foam/batting section, batting-side-down, onto the wrong side of the fabric. Gently but firmly, pull the fabric onto the plywood and attach with one staple centered on each side.

7 *Stapling, continued*

For tailored cushions: Work around the cushion, adding staples equally on all sides. Keep the pressure even.

For shirred cushions: Don't staple the fabric at the sides yet, only at the top and bottom.

Occasionally turn the cushion to the front side and organize the gathers.

Staple the sides, with the fabric pulled taut. Pulling the fabric too tightly will disturb the gathers.

8 *Corners*

For all cushions: To make a neat corner, cut the point off the corner. Tuck one point into the overlap. Then fold the remaining point under. Staple in place.

9 *Finishing*

For all cushions: Find the fabric set aside for covering the back of the cushion. Fold and press the edges 2 in. (5 cm) to the wrong side.

To make a neat corner, notch the corner nearly to the crease. Fold one edge flat. Then fold the other edge over it, tucking the corner under.

For a flat finish: Heat up the glue gun. *Be careful not to burn your fingers, especially if you are not experienced with a glue gun.* The glue becomes hot enough to cause deep burns, and the glue sticks and keeps burning.

Position the fabric, centered onto the back of the cushion, right-side-up. Pin at the corners. Unpin and lift one corner. With the glue gun at high heat, squeeze a narrow, neat bead just inside the folded edge of the fabric. Lay the corner down, allow the glue to cool and lift the next corner. Repeat until the back is glued on all the way around.

10 *Finishing, continued*

For a trimmed finish: Plug in the glue gun. Lay the fabric centered onto the back of the cushion, right-side-up. Staple the fabric to the back of the cushion, centering one staple on each of the four sides. Staples must be carefully placed at the edge of the fold of the fabric. Otherwise, they will not be covered by the trim. Work out from the positioning staples equally, stapling along the edges of the fabric on all four sides.

Wrap a small piece of tape around the end of the braid to prevent fraying. Carefully apply hot glue to the taped end of the braid, then slip this end under the edge of the fabric between two staples, hiding the tape. Working in sections, apply a bead of hot glue to the underside of the braid and lay the braid glue-side-down, hiding the staples and the folded edge of the fabric.

When the braid is glued on all the way around, cut it with 1 in. (2.5 cm) excess. Tape around the end. Apply glue to the end and tuck it into the gap with the other end, keeping the join as invisible as possible.

11 *Reattaching cushions*

For all cushions: In a color compatible with the fabric, paint the heads of the screws to be used for reattaching the seat.

Position the seat back into the chair. Mark where the screw holes will go.

Using a sharp utility knife or X-acto knife, cut a tiny hole at each of the marks. The cut should break only one or two threads, allowing the screws to pass through the fabric. If these holes are not cut, the fabric will bunch when the screws are screwed in.

Position the seat back in place and screw in the screws.

JOY VON TIEDEMANN

SHEILA McGRAW began her career painting sets and
designing props for major high-fashion retailers. She then moved into the
highly competitive world of freelance illustration, producing art for
newspapers, magazines, advertising and package design. Next she turned to
illustrating children's books. Her first book, Robert Munsch's *Love You Forever*,
became an international bestseller that reached number one on the
New York Times Children's Bestseller List.

An avid home sewer, decorator and painter, she has written numerous craft
books, including *Papier-Mâché for Kids*, a bestseller that won the prestigious
Benjamin Franklin Award. Her books on painted and decorated furniture have
firmly established her as one of the foremost writers in the field.
Sheila McGraw lives on a farm north of Toronto and is
the mother of three grown sons.

BOOKS WRITTEN BY SHEILA McGRAW

Papier-Mâché Today; Papier-Mâché for Kids;
Soft Toys to Sew; Gifts Kids Can Make;
Dolls Kids Can Make; Pussycats Everywhere;
This Old New House; Painting and Decorating Furniture;
Decorating Furniture: Antique and Country Paint Projects; Decorating
Furniture: Découpage, Paint and Fabric Projects; Decorating Furniture: Stencil,
Paint and Block Print Projects; Decorating Furniture: Texture,
Paint, Ornament and Mosaic Projects

BOOKS ILLUSTRATED BY SHEILA McGRAW

Love You Forever, I Promise I'll Find You, Lightning Bug Thunder